I DIDN'T REALLY KNOW

Him

I Didn't Really Know Him

A Memoir

Fauneil Fremont

Xulon Elite

Xulon Press Elite
2301 Lucien Way #415
Maitland, FL 32751
407.339.4217
www.xulonpress.com

Unless otherwise indicated, Scripture quotations taken from the Holy Bible, New International Version (NIV). Copyright © 1973, 1978, 1984, 2011 by Biblica, Inc.™. Used by permission. All rights reserved.

Printed in the United States of America.

ISBN-13: 978-1-54567-462-8

TABLE OF CONTENTS

ACKNOWLEDGMENTS

I extend my thanks and appreciation to

my late husband, whose poetry I have used,

my niece, who supported me emotionally during my husband's cancer, his death, and the months following,

my daughter and children, who are attentive to my needs as I adjust to a new way of life,

the clergy for spiritual care,
and to my friend who encouraged me to write.

Chapter 1

INTRODUCTION

To the Reader from the Author:
My late husband's poems, autobiographical sketches, and quotes from his father's memoirs are verbatim. Also, all historical facts, place names, and time periods are nonfiction.

The names of all characters and incidental names are fictional. I chose to tell the story with "Beth" as the narrator to avoid becoming too emotional as I relayed experiences of a fifty-seven-year marriage. Also, I wanted to present "Will" as objectively as possible.

The STORY:

To understand why I, Beth, at age twenty-five married a young Englishman named Will, whom I didn't really know, you must know something about my background. At age twenty-five in 1960, I was still relatively naïve.

Until I was in the fifth grade, my parents and we three girls—Nancy, Elizabeth (Beth), and Amy—had lived in Hoskins, a very small rural village in northeastern Nebraska. It was the same community where my grandparents and my great-grandparents had lived after they emigrated from Germany. I grew up with their stories of the hardship of life on a prairie, drought, and the Great Depression. My ancestors had been rugged, hardworking, goal-centered people who had a belief in God and a strong desire to make life better for the next generation.

My sister Nancy and I, being only fifteen months apart in age, were best "buddies" as we wandered about Hoskins during our childhood. When Mom was taking Dad's place at the rural bank during his hail-adjusting trips, we were looked after by Agatha, a middle-aged spinster. Doting on baby Amy, she allowed us older girls to leave the house for unsupervised times. We wandered about the village, sneaking into an old, abandoned hotel, stopping by to say hi to the postmistress, and going into the schoolyard to get water from the outdoor pump to make mud for our bee stings. Near home, we picked wild grapes growing alongside the road, looked for crawdads in a nearby stream, and discussed how to rescue a rabbit that had fallen into a dry well.

Nancy, the big sister, was always protective of me. As we roamed, she warned me about poison oak or a rut-hole in the dirt road. Later when I was near death during my early years of marriage, she flew from Nebraska to Washington, D.C., to watch at my bedside. To this day, she has remained the concerned older sister.

Our parents raised us to have no fear of the future. Married in 1932 during the Great Depression, they had struggled to provide food and shelter for their family. Mom remade clothes for us from hand-me-downs given to her by a neighbor lady. She baked bread each day; she canned meat, fruits, and vegetables that Grandmother had brought in from her farm; she kept a clean house even though the only running water available was from the kitchen pump.

Dad, too, was very hardworking but humble enough to accept any work that could help his family. One winter season when the snow was blocking the businesses all over town, Dad scooped snow from morning until night, making a total of thirty cents a day, enough to buy flour for bread. Before moving into town, he had tried farming on Grandmother's land, but a relentless drought had forced him back to town. With his brother, they opened a small grocery store. The farmers came into town on the weekends to sell their chickens, eggs, milk, and cream. Dad gave them credit for each item and then allowed them to purchase fruits, vegetables, and staples from the store.

When the Depression began to lift, the bank reopened, and farmers needed crop adjustors to evaluate their losses after it hailed. Next, Dad started an insurance and real estate business. When World War II began, the economy began booming. Dad and Mom moved our family to the larger town of Norfolk, fifteen miles away from Hoskins. They wanted us three girls to have more advantages in education and music and Dad to have more opportunities in business.

Except for the first year of adjusting to a new community, I was a happy child and teenager, excelling in school and piano performance. I earned a scholarship to the University of Nebraska. Upon graduating in 1956, I joined a study group for a summer trip to Europe, borrowing the money from my father, which I repaid during my first year of teaching English in Tucson, Arizona. While teaching I attended the University of Arizona as a student at night. During the summers, I became a full-time student until I earned my M.Ed. degree in 1959.

During my final summer at the U of A, I met Frank, who was finishing an MBA degree. We fell in love and soon became promised to each other. My mother had strongly advised each of her three girls to remain virgins until marriage. My father, however, had often advised us to be open and loving. I took his advice. Frank was a gentle lover. He did not satisfy his own needs in love-making at the expense of his partner.

Frank wanted to start his career in San Jose, California. I joined him there after acquiring a teaching position in a high school for the coming year. Though engaged, we did not live together before marriage. (In 1959, many girls tried to follow the adage, "First the engagement, then the marriage, then the baby carriage.") However, the engagement didn't work out, and by January 1959, I began to think that I would end up an "old maid" schoolteacher, like my mother's aunt had unhappily called herself.

Will, a charming and witty Englishman, and I met in February 1960 at the apartment complex where we both lived. We were only casual friends for six months. I talked about teaching English while he was centered on Mary, his girlfriend from L.A. Our dating relationship began in August after our encounter at the swimming pool of the complex. Will was playing bridge by the side of the pool. When the fourth player left, Will asked me to join them. I was wearing a baby blue one-piece bathing suit with tiny buttons in front. I could tell from his look that he found my 34-24-34 figure attractive.

Will liked to talk about himself, and within the next two weeks I learned everything about him that *he* wanted me to know. He had grown up in Peterborough, England, where one of the old Norman cathedrals dominated the town and its central square. His mother and father were bookkeepers, she in a florist's shop and he in a brick company.

His mother was the oldest in a family of eight girls, and Will became the *first male child* in the family for years. He had been christened with an important-sounding name, William Parker Hayes, worthy of his place in the family. He had been the favorite grandchild of his grandfather, a prominent detective in the Peterborough police. Through his grandfather and his parents, Will had received the best schooling available in the area at the Deacon's School for Boys. At age nine, when Will was dangerously ill with encephalitis and rheumatic fever, his parents had provided him with private medical treatment and care for six months.

At age seventeen, Will matriculated to the University of London, to an outlying branch in Leicester. He studied pure math and physics and was in the top group of ten students during his first year. A physics professor was worried about Will's intensity and suggested that he take up a hobby for relaxation. Will started fencing and playing bridge, which became an addiction. (Bridge is a trick-taking card game using a fifty-two-card deck. It is played by four people in two competing partnerships. The two variations of the game are rubber or social bridge and duplicate bridge, used in tournament play. The partners first bid to make a contract before the play begins.)

Will played bridge with fellow students hour after hour, often skipping professors' lectures or studying. He felt, like George Bernard Shaw, that bridge was "the most entertaining and intelligent game the wit of man" has invented. Therefore, two years later, when he received a third-class degree instead of a first-class one, he was not surprised. However, he blamed his physics professor for removing him from the top group of ten students.

Upon graduating, he was hired as an aeronautical engineering trainee at Vickers Super Marine, an airplane company in Southampton, England, where he remained for three years. I learned that he had been in Southampton when my ship docked there in the summer of 1956. We could have met at that time if our paths had crossed.

Will decided to immigrate to Toronto, Canada, by the end of that summer for a better-paying position as a stress engineer at Avro Aircraft. In Toronto he moved into a house with four other bachelor roommates. They were intelligent young men who shared his interests in bridge, reading, writing, traveling, and classical music. Will auditioned for and became a member of the famous Toronto Mendelssohn Choir. In England he had studied voice and violin and was well trained for the performances the choir gave.

In 1959 Will emigrated to the U.S., taking work in temporary job-shop situations to allow himself more freedom to go skiing. After a year of this, he moved to L.A., where he was trained in computers by IBM, who then sent him to their branch in San Jose.

Will had been selective in what he had told me about himself. After we were married, I learned that he was a very complicated person, but his inner personality partly revealed itself only gradually throughout our fifty-seven years of marriage. Following his death, when I searched for biographical information about him, I discovered more than I expected to find.

Chapter 2

GETTING TO KNOW YOU

S ince Will had portrayed himself as a somewhat naïve, inexperienced lover when we were
engaged, I was surprised after his death to find the poem
"Farewell," written by a coworker at Avro Aircraft in
Toronto. Will had tucked it away in a reference book
that we seldom used.

> *Farewell, my Will—Fate indeed is cruel*
> *To prise from Avro's Crown so fair a Jewel,*
> *A Gem of many facets, polished fair—*
> *Oh! never did we see a bird so rare.*
> *Stress, Music, Aerodynamics, Maths,*
> *Surefooted he on all these divers' paths;*
> *Poetry, too. Surely if his endeavor*
> *Was centred on one Goal, I should think never*
> *Were Laurels quite so handy to be clutched.*

Why, many have I heard say, "Is he touched
by Genius?" Ah! fortunate my way
To work with such a colleague day by day.

Have patience with me, friends, do not bewail
If I am prolix; truly I would fail
To do him justice if I did not mention
His way with ladies. Never, do I think
Has man stepped so surefooted on the brink
of Matrimony. And yet when romance ends
The lady counts him still amongst her friends.
He always seems sincere upon his part—
He is a Cunning Dog, he knows the Art
Of Love from Ovid via Marie Stopes,
Clean through to Kinsey—yes—he knows the ropes
To woo so many, yet stay clear of Marriage.
Yet mark you this, I mean not to disparage
His Honour or intentions, - 'tis not done,
And much that I have said is said in fun.
But truly now—we hate to see you leave
And if we do not seem to deeply grieve
Your leaving us is not so sweet a sorrow—
Let's hope for your return some fair to-morrow.

Barry, Jan. 1959, Toronto

Barry described here some of Will's traits: (1) His "Genius"—Will proudly acknowledged that his IQ was in the 160s. (2) His lack of centering on one "Goal"—If he had concentrated on his studies in math and physics at the University of London, he could have gotten a First Class Degree. (3) A "Cunning Dog"—To charm the ladies, Will knew how to flirt with words, accents, and gestures. (4) The "Art of Love"—He often wrote poems to intensify a relationship.

Even though AIDS was relatively unknown in 1959, other consequences of promiscuity were there, but Will knew how to protect himself with condoms, and young women were beginning to wear diaphragms. Yes, Will was ready for the ski slopes of Colorado and the lifestyle of the "skiing crowd."

Will had gotten a taste of skiing in Canada. He was ready for a change from that of a serious young man with an interest in his work to one who works only enough to pay for pleasure. If his parents had known that he was leaving Canada for the sport of skiing, they would have been very worried and displeased. Skiing is a dangerous sport and taxing for the body, especially for a heart with a leaky valve, the result of his rheumatic fever at age nine. In England, his parents had been very careful that he had not physically overexerted himself, but Will was a "clever dog." His parents were far away and did not need to know about his lifestyle.

Will left his secure position at Avro Aircraft for a job-shop situation in Denver, Colorado. Living in Denver, Aurora, and then Colorado Springs, he had access to different ski slopes throughout the long winter months. This was the time when he wrote most of his poems of passion. He seemed to fall in love every month with a different girl, writing to and wooing Gisela in January, Joan in February, Jane in March, Carol in April and May, Joan again in July, Janice in August. In his June poem (no name given), he summed up his passion:

My love is like a flaming fire,
That feeds the flames of my desire,
And burns upon the funeral pyre
Of my lost bachelorhood.

In his poem "Ski Colorado," he described the skiing lifestyle as "a way of life unto itself":

What is skiing?
To ski is to fly like a bird, to ski

14

Is to encounter speed in the raw, to ski
Is to begin to live dangerously and to revel
In near brushes with disaster. Skiing is
A special kind of individual physical freedom,
A new way of escaping from the stresses of life
And the best way to fill your lungs with
Vitalizing mountain air. And of the camaraderie
Of skiers who can write. Of the pale beer,
The dark beer, the bawdy songs, the libido
And its fulfilment in a way not wanton,
But with the shared satisfaction of healthy sex.
To ski Colorado is a way of life unto itself.

Colorado Springs, June 9, 1959

When I discovered these poems after his death, I almost chuckled at the ridiculousness of his "lost bachelorhood." With so many different partners, he must have become quite experienced.

When there was no more work available in the job-shop area, Will, Sam (a skiing buddy), and Carol drove to L.A., where Will applied to IBM for computer training. Because his job would not begin until

September, the three friends drove to Ensenada, Mexico, for a holiday. Carol was a girlfriend to both Sam and to Will, as evidenced by Will's poem to Carol about his "willingness to share her."

If I can't have you to myself alone,
Then I'll be content to share you—
All your errant waywardness condone,
And any jealousy I'll spare you.

I need your kind of laughter and your wit;
I need your happy, carefree air;
I love to tease you when alone we sit;
I think we'd make a wholesome pair.

And still I will forget the other men
Whose lives you share as well as mine—
And if I count them up and find us ten,
I'll find some way to lose the nine.

April 14, 1959

By the end of the vacation, Carol went off with Sam, and Will began training at IBM. On their entrance exam, he had gotten the most points ever scored by candidates. He had a promising beginning; IBM expected continued achievement from him.

However, skiing season began again in late October, and Will headed for the slopes near L.A. and Whittier. After work on a Friday, he drove into the mountains, skied all weekend, and returned late on Sunday evening. His manager reported that it took Will three days to perform well at work because he was so tired. Not wanting to lose the promise that Will had first shown, IBM moved him to San Jose, California, in February 1960. Will did not get their message to improve. The ski slopes of the Sierra Nevada Mountains were only five hours away.

Will left behind his girlfriend, Mary, a programmer at IBM in L.A. She doesn't appear to have been a skier, but she was apparently pretty, intelligent, and appreciative of his mathematical, logical mind—someone who finally understood his "genius." Will wrote love poems to her until the end of March, when he learned that separation of being miles apart had not increased their romance.

I need you, how I need you,
And we're many miles apart.
I want to kiss you and hold you,
Caressingly enfold you—
I never yet have told you
That we must never part.

O let me hold you,
Let me embrace you,
Kissing away all your cares and fears;
Lovingly tend you
And tenderly love you,
Whispering love's message so soft in your ears.

March, 1960

At the beginning of August, Will was given a bad performance review and then fired. This was a wake-up call for him. He had no income; he had accumulated much debt from the expensive sport of skiing and his trip to Mexico, and his parents were arriving from England in two weeks. Also, there was the fear of being deported as an unemployed noncitizen. What could he do? How could he appear to his parents as the serious young man of promise they thought him to be?

His solution was to begin dating me daily and eagerly during the next two weeks. I was flattered with so much attention from an Englishman, who was so unlike any of the Americans I had dated. Shortly after his parents arrived, I showed them American hospitality by inviting them to dinner. I prepared a meal that I knew the English always enjoyed: roast beef with Yorkshire pudding, roasted potatoes and carrots, and trifle for dessert.

After dinner, his mother, Laura, helped me with dishes in the kitchen while Will took his father, Clyde, for a walk. Will later reported to me that his father had been very impressed with me and had said, "If you don't marry that girl, you're a damned fool." Will convinced his father that we were well on our way to a lasting relationship: we had been dating since February, we had been playing violin and piano together, I had a good-paying job, as did he, and we were both ready for marriage. The deception continued. In spite of Will's debt, he played the grand host by taking his parents on a sightseeing car trip to Yosemite and Zion Parks, the Grand Canyon, L.A. and north on Highway One through Carmel and Monterey. Finally, he drove them across the U.S. to New York City, where they boarded the *Queen Elizabeth* for an ocean trip back to England. At the time, I thought Will had been a dutiful son and had saved up much of his salary for this trip.

After Will returned to San Jose in late September, he found work immediately as a mathematician at Food Machinery Corporation (FMC). In looking through old employment documents, which I found after his death, I began to see his frequent changes in employment. Barry at Avro in Toronto had been right. Will had not centered on a "Goal."

In 1960, however, Will was centered on marrying me. Economically I was a good "catch." I was in my fifth year of teaching, had earned two degrees, and had lived a life of moderation and frugality. My lifestyle was totally unlike that of his former ski amours.

Our engagement was short—engaged in mid-October on Will's birthday and married on December 25. We shopped together for the diamond ring. (I did not question why a twenty-eight-year-old man, after working for seven and a half years, would need to pay for the ring on a layaway plan.) There was no romantic celebration of this important occasion—no flowers or champagne, no poem presented to me. I later found among his poems one that was addressed to "My Wife-to-be":

Will you be girlfriend, oh girl of brown hair,
Or will you waltz past me with nose in the air?
Will you be sweetheart, my lass of fair face,
Or do I plead vainly my love-sick case?
Will you be lover, and lend me your charms,
Or scorning, refuse to lie in my arms?
Will you be promised and accept my ring,
Or will you reject my fond offering?

December, 1960

In one of his books of poems I found after he died, I came across a much more elevated expression of love, which he had written in January, 1960, before we had met. With its three-syllable and four-syllable words, the poem must have been written to Mary, whom he considered highly intelligent.

Know my heart, my love . . .
The faint, eager heart of the young,
Who know all, yet know nothing:
Whose experience is the quick sudden surge

of intermittent comprehension,
The dawning of a pale luminary,
The twinkling of a third magnitude star.

Two other poems Will wrote in December 1960 were ones he must have hastily jotted down. I found them fifty-eight years later:

Vows
Vows I make
I'll never break.
Or else those vows
I'd never take.

December 25
Bride to be: Love me
As I love thee.
Happy pair, with care
We well will wear.

December, 1960

Chapter 3

MARRIAGE AND BIRTH

*A*fter his death, when I read the autobiographical sketches Will had left on his computer, I was surprised at his omissions. Who wouldn't consider his/her wedding day as an occasion for remembrance? (He did, however, leave a very detailed description of each of his seven failed attempts to get a driver's license in Toronto, followed by the final success of the eighth attempt.)

I remember well our wedding day! It was a beautiful Christmas Day, in 1960, in Nebraska. A light snow was falling and colorful lights were everywhere. No decorations inside the church were needed—the trees and poinsettias were still there from the morning service. My two sisters wore green velvet gowns, and I had purchased for myself a white heavy taffeta gown with tiny covered buttons down the back. The gown was not fussy but elegant, purchased in San Francisco at the expensive I. Magnin Store. At twenty-five, I had insisted on paying for my own gown.

My parents and grandmother provided the rest. I had left the planning of the pre-wedding dinner, the wedding itself, and the reception following to my mother because she and Dad had never had a formal wedding. They had eloped in 1932 during the Great Depression rather than subject their families to expense. My grandmother, at age seventy-five, prepared dinner in her home for the entire wedding party. She took an immediate liking to my charming Englishman with his strange accent. It was a wonderful, delightful affair, and Will was heartily welcomed into the family.

A low point of the wedding day for me was Will's non-reaction to seeing me in my wedding gown—no light of love in his eyes, no whispered "You're beautiful." My father, perhaps sensing my disappointment, gave me an enormous hug after the ceremony. The photographer snapped a picture of us just as rays of light streamed down upon us.

Our wedding night, in a hotel in Grand Island, was unconsummated. Will was not feeling well, although he had not seemed ill earlier. The sickness continued into the next day. He did not apologize; he was simply quiet—a prelude to life ahead.

Throughout his life, Will often wrote poems or ditties about suffering, longing, or sickness. His ditty from March 21, 1960, might have been written on our wedding night:

O where is all the spirit now?
Where is all the cheer?
Where is all the festive cup?
I've spewed it up, I fear.

The next day, sick Will and I were headed by car for Aspen, Colorado, to go skiing. Will had chosen a skiing resort for our honeymoon even though I had never been on skis. "You'll learn fast," he had assured me. In the 1960s the honeymoon was still considered the responsibility of the bridegroom. I had allowed Will to make all the arrangements, and I was imagining a romantic ambience: a cabin retreat with a fire glowing in a large stone fireplace, flowers and champagne awaiting our arrival.

What a shock I felt as we entered the kitchen of a smelly, tacky fishing cabin: linoleum on the floor, an old stove and refrigerator available, a wall heater instead of a fireplace, and an old narrow double bed, comfortable only for one. I couldn't help blurting out, "If you expect me to cook, you're crazy!" Another night absent of intimacy followed. Will slept in the narrow bed; I took the battered fake leather couch.

I am reminded of lines from a poem addressed to Gisela:

If you ever meet a woman whom you can admire,
Cleave to her.
She is noble and true because your love for her
Will be of the highest and purest kind.
She is yours—
And your only difficulty is to convince her
That you do need her.

There was an awfully lot of convincing that was needed between the two of us. I felt that I was not worthy enough to merit a sensitive, loving beginning. Instead, Will expected me to be a good sport, ready to go fishing if the lakes had not been frozen.

The next day we started anew. Intimacy at night followed daytime fun. A large stone fireplace in the gathering room provided a cheery blaze and much-needed atmosphere for love. We both enjoyed the camaraderie of other young couples, some who were also honeymooners.

Will was surprised that I needed only one day on the bunny slope before I was ready for the intermediate slope. I had been active in sports: swimming, tennis, skating and sledding, square dancing, and a daily routine of morning exercises. Also, my lifestyle of moderation had paid off.

On the intermediate slope, my biggest problem was how to stop without sometimes falling. After one fall, Will stopped to help me up and then immediately pushed me sideways into the snowbank, as a lesson in falling. I was angry at this aggressive treatment. Had I married a bully? In the years to come, he retold this incident often, enjoying the "humor" of it.

A month after we returned home to San Jose, we had an argument about money. Will was too impatient to resolve the issue with discussion. He forced me over his knees and spanked me like a naughty child. I ran out of the apartment and intended to leave permanently. My mother had warned me to not allow myself to be treated "like a dishrag." My father and she had always treated each other with mutual respect. But she had told me stories about her father-in-law, with his quick temper, who had beaten his wife even though she had borne him twelve children. Finally, she had run away from home, and he had begged her to come back, promising to keep his temper under control.

Likewise, Will came after me and cajoled me to return. I gave in but warned him that that was the last time I would allow myself to be struck. Many times in the following years, he was angry enough to raise his hand, but he didn't follow through.

Will and I had only been married for seven weeks when our daughter Dora was conceived. We had gone to Squaw Valley to ski for the Lincoln Holiday weekend. We skied a little the first day, but then a blizzard arose and we became trapped inside our room. There was no television, and we had not bothered to bring books with us. Suddenly, with no romantic buildup, Will said, "Let's make a baby."

As I recall our early days, I realize that becoming a father was more of a priority for Will than being a lover to me. We had not yet discussed parenthood. During our engagement period, we had both talked about our childhood illnesses. He had described being very sick for a year but had failed to tell me that he had been left with a scarred aortic heart valve, evidenced by a heart murmur. (In 1961 open-heart surgery was not yet an answer to the problem.) Will had been told that his scarred heart valve would become a severe medical problem and that he should not expect to live a long life. When I learned this later in our marriage, I felt cheated that he had not shared this information with me before we were married. After just seven weeks of marriage, I could not know why he was so anxious to "make" a baby!

After his death, when I read his poem "The Bund-a-ling," written in February 1960, I realized that he had wanted a likeness of self when he was dating Mary.

I dreamed last night
That you did wear my wedding ring;
That you knew well a prettier thing.

There was nearby a tiny child, a pretty thing
That came from us, a bund-a-ling.
I thought I heard my pretty sing
A lullaby—an offering.
The baby held a teething ring.

And then the cruel night did fling
The curtain back and ended
My wishful thinking.

29

When I read that after his death, I was touched by the tenderness of the poem, but I didn't like imagining a union of Will and Mary producing a baby who would have been quite different from our Dora.

Being newly married and busy as an English teacher, I had not really thought much about motherhood. I wanted to be wooed and romanced and loved for myself. I wanted time to learn to better know the man I had married.

I was miserable with morning sickness during the remainder of the school term. My body was rapidly changing internally and then finally externally. I wanted to be asked, "Can I get you something?" Or I wanted to be told, "You look beautiful to me" or "I hope the baby has your lovely blue eyes, Beth." Still, that last imaginary comment would have been unlikely. Will had often commented on how women had complimented him on his own blue eyes.

When our adorable Dora was born, I thought that surely she had replaced Will's longing for his old flame. However, after he returned from a business trip to L.A., he told me he had looked up Mary to show her pictures of the baby and me. I couldn't believe he had done this. When I questioned him about it, he called me "jealous." Since my parents were visiting us at the time, we did not pursue the issue. They had stayed for a week following Dora's birth, with my mother helping me around the house so that I could recuperate from the birth, and my dad enjoying watching his daughter becoming a mother. Before they left, Dad snapped a photo of Will with his arm around me as I held Dora on the front steps of our house—a picture of tender love.

For the next six months, tenderness and loving feelings continued among the three of us. Will wrote two sweet poems at this time, which he shared with me:

The Newcomer

Little wife comes home tomorrow,
    Bringin' baby home as well—
Little wife I love so dearly:
    Love her more than I can tell.
Now two sweet ones I have love for—
    Little wife and babe as well;
Darling wife I love so dearly,
    Love her more than I can tell.
'Neath one roof we'll live together,
    And our little dog as well.
For our daughter then a brother!
    And another "gal" as well!

In my fam'ly I take pleasure—
  In my fam'ly pride as well;
In my wife who loves me dearly,
  Pride and pleasure blend so well.

Who's This Little Stranger?

Who's this little stranger
  That's not a little stranger anymore?
She's the sweetest little baby
  That San Jose or California ever saw:
At three months old she smiles and coos
  And very nearly talks—
She almost sits, and almost stands
  And darned near even walks.

Fate was unkind. Dreams of a brother and sister for Dora were not to be. When I gave birth to Dora, a part of the afterbirth remained imbedded so deeply within the walls of the uterus that the doctor could not remove it, although he finally yanked out (painfully for me) what he thought was all of it. However, small, unseen portions remained. In the ensuing months, it developed into a hydatidiform mole. My uterus thought it was still feeding a developing fetus, supplying it with continual nourishment and blood. The mole grew so rapidly I looked like I was carrying twins within a few months. The doctor was convinced that I was pregnant again even though I was nursing Dora.

By the end of May 1962, Will was sent to Washington, D.C., by Control Data Corporation to work on a three-month project. He managed to find a way so that Dora and I could accompany him. We had been in D.C. for only a few weeks before I began to have massive hemorrhages. A doctor at Prince George's Hospital diagnosed my case correctly, and I was taken in for an emergency hysterotomy within a few hours.

My heart was so enlarged from the months of trying to supply blood that the surgeons had to perform the operation with localized anesthesia via needles into the abdomen. As I lay on the operating table, I could not feel my abdomen, but I could hear the surgeons preparing for surgery, swathing the area, cutting open the abdomen and then the uterus. I heard one of them gasp as he removed the mole. I caught a glimpse of a cluster of what looked like white grapes before it fell apart.

I felt my heart pounding violently. Suddenly I couldn't breathe. As I suffered heart failure, my head felt like it was gyrating rapidly back and forth. Then my spirit escaped from my body and I experienced rapidly being propelled through a long, dark tunnel. Finally, the tunnel ended, and I was alone in the darkness. It seemed like I was in a "no-man's-space" with nothing but my own thoughts. Like others have said, there is time now to reflect on all of the past, even insignificant words or deeds that one has long forgotten. After the period of reflection, I felt the loneliness of knowing that I could be here alone with only my own thoughts for all of eternity. The fear of eternal solitude and of waiting were unbearable. I finally cried out, "God, help me!"

Immediately an extremely bright, warm, comforting light appeared. I knew that God was there. Although the light and I conversed, it was an unspoken conversation. I begged the light to allow me to go back to care for my child. I knew, without being told, that if I stayed, I would enter the light I could see all around me. If I were sent back, it would be not only to care for Dora but for reasons that I could not understand at the time.

Gradually, I felt my spirit returning to join my body. Although frightening, the feeling of being only a spirit had been free and light in comparison with the heaviness of gravity I felt as my spirit reunited with my body. I found myself again struggling for each breath. I did not know that they had restarted my heart on the operating table, had given me pints and pints of blood, and finally had succeeded in bringing me back to the land of the living. Then they had transferred me to intensive care and put me into an oxygen tent.

Meanwhile, Will had been waiting with anxiety and fear, first at the hospital and then throughout the coming weeks as I did not recover. He expressed his feelings in his poem called "Waiting."

Under the Washington sky without you,
Not any pleasure, and no-one to woo,
Easy to see why I married you, dear,
I'm never alone when I have you near.
God gave me you to share the long, still hours,
Sweet scent of pleasure, the perfume of flow'rs.
Now I fear to close my eyes in my gloom;
Listless I wait near the phone in my room.
Hundreds of minutes with nothing to do,
Suffering the pain of waiting for you.

I was in the hospital in D.C. during June and July while Mother took care of Dora. My sister Donna flew from Nebraska to stay at my bedside. Somehow she must have known that she would be needed to save me. One afternoon while Will was sitting and reading in my room, Donna was watching closely at my bedside. A nurse came into the room and changed the oxygen canister, but she forgot to turn back on the oxygen machine. Donna watched as my breathing became more and more labored. Finally, she turned to Will and said, "There's something wrong. The little red ball should be jumping up and down, and Beth is breathing her own carbon dioxide." "Don't be silly, Donna," Will responded. "The nurses know what they're doing." Donna ignored him and ran out to the nurses' station, demanding a nurse come immediately. Will was gracious enough to admit that he had been wrong, deadly wrong.

By the end of July, I was able to travel to my parents' home in Nebraska, where further surgeries were performed in the Lutheran Hospital, the last one being a combination hysterectomy/ovariectomy when the doctor discovered that choriocarcinoma had developed. Will stayed in Washington until his project had been completed. During this time, he wrote his touching poem, "The Summer of '62":

Honey, Honey,—O Beth my sweet Honey,
I'm watching and waiting and praying for you—
Dull ache within me—I'm fighting my fears:
How slim the chance you will live!
As each minute passes, I add thirty more—
Doctor and surgeon arrive looking stern;
It's done!—"though she's not out of danger."
Long hours now, the fam'ly vigil of love:
 Oxygen tent with no oxygen flow!
 Running a fever not once, but ten times,
 Antiseptic shots, pints of blood by the score.
Minutes and hours pass to days and to weeks,
In—out of urgent care many more times—
Leave you I must...to another "white coat."
End of the summer.....but no end to this!

When I was released from the hospital, I was reunited with Dora, who had learned to walk at Mom and Dad's home. At first she thought I was a stranger. I said to Mom, "She thinks you're her mother now." Mother assured me that Dora would remember me as her mother as soon as I began to take care of her again. I started to try to bond with Dora again by taking her for walks in her stroller. It was already fall. A cold snap had occurred, causing the beautiful Nebraska leaves to turn golden and red and to begin to fall. As we walked, the wheels of the baby carriage crunched the leaves. "Listen to the leaves, Dora," I said. "They're saying *Crunch, Crunch*. I remember you."

This short golden period had to end when my chemotherapy was started. In 1962 cancer was just beginning to be followed up by a new treatment of drugs. My doctor prescribed a five-month treatment of Methotrexate. But because the chances of my surviving it were slim, he sent me home to California with Dora for my last days with Will.

Chapter 4

RECOVERY

I finally flew home with Dora to San Jose in mid-September and was placed under the care of doctors there for further treatment and observation. I wish I could remember much that happened during the next four months, but I was too sick to do more than daily survive and care for Dora.

I only remember vividly one beautiful experience when Dora was about eleven months old and was becoming adept at walking. She was in my care. I became extremely tired in the afternoon and badly needed a nap. I fed her, gave her a glass of milk, changed her diaper, gathered up some of her toys, fetched our dog, Fritz, and enclosed us in a small guest bedroom, making sure the door was secure. The room was bare except for a carpet on the floor and a hide-a-bed. When

Dora was busy with her play, I settled on the couch and fell into a deep sleep. When I awoke hours later, I found that Dora had crawled up onto the couch and had stretched herself across me, nestling her head against my neck. What a precious moment!

Holes in my memory of the days from September through January were never filled by anything Will wrote at the time or later. I do not know when he went to work or when he came home. Did he take care of meals? Did he do laundry, clean bathrooms, vacuum, feed the dog, care for Dora, entertain himself, or communicate with my parents or his?

From an entry in his father's memoirs, I gathered that there had been little communication to his parents about the summer and fall of 1962. Clyde wrote, *"Their daughter was born in November. There was to be another addition to the family the next year, but something went wrong, and she was not able to have any more children, so Dora is the one and only."* (If there had been better communication, perhaps a future family tragedy could have been avoided.)

By the end of January 1963, my chemotherapy was over, and I was beginning to feel better and stronger each day. The cancer had been arrested, but it would be five years before it could be termed conquered. I was thankful for each new day. I loved being in our humble little home and taking care of our precious toddler. When spring and then summer arrived, I took Dora for daily walks in the sunshine, accompanied by Fritz.

My bubble of happiness burst at the end of July. Will, like his whimsical character, Tommy Titmouse, wanted a bigger house:

Little Tommy Titmouse
Didn't know what to do—
He had a very tiny house,
Just big enough for two.

Then one morning she said,
His little wife, said she,
As she lay snug in bed,
"Tomorrow there'll be three."

There was just nothing for it—
If that really was the case—
He'd have to hunt around a bit,
And find a bigger place!

(Will was very proud of this bit of whimsy and quoted it often to others in later life, even though it evoked for me, standing nearby, such unpleasant memories.) Will and his mother, Laura, had been communicating about plans for his parents to come to California to live with us when Clyde retired in September, 1964. Clyde wrote in his memoirs: "*Will suggested that when I reached sixty-five, I should retire from the Brick Company. He would build a house large enough, so that we could have our own apartments with a family room, where we could get together at times.*" This was an impossible plan. Will knew that he could not build a large house on his salary. I would need to go back to teaching, and he had not shared the plan with me. Also, his parents could not leisurely enjoy their own apartment within the house. We could not afford to employ a maid, a babysitter, and a gardener out of my teacher's salary. Will's actual plan was that I would teach, Clyde would become the gardener, and Laura would become the housekeeper and babysitter. Clyde was certainly unaware of the real plan.

Both Will and his mother were strong-willed, stubborn people, accustomed to getting their way. In the next year, Clyde and Laura sold their home, furniture, and many of their personal belongings. They packed only the items they would move to their new apartment in America. Then they took all of the economic and governmental steps needed for their visas and future security.

Will searched for a building site, escorted me to meet with prospective builders, and encouraged me to participate in the design of and materials for the house. He also found a future temporary babysitter for Dora. I was on my own to find a teaching job in August. I was hoping that it was too late to find work, but unfortunately I obtained a position as an English teacher in a high school in San Jose just in time for the opening of the school year in September.

The first day of school was heartbreaking for both Dora and me. The babysitter lived in the direction of Will's work, and my school was the opposite way. I remember Dora screaming as Will had to force her from my arms. She was still reaching out to me as he walked through the doorway. I was devastated. I had missed three months of her babyhood when I was in the hospital. Dora and I had had only seven months together since the end of my chemotherapy.

I realized that Will had made life-altering choices. He had chosen his mother to replace me to raise our child. He had chosen her needs over mine or those of our daughter. I felt like the "dishrag" my own mother had warned me not to become. Will, however, was as happy as a lark with the plan that had been hatched. For him, the world was spinning merrily along as the sun and the moon sailed through space:

The Sun and the Moon

The sun and moon in the sky
Must have learned in the past how to fly;
They go sailing through space at a phenomenal pace,
Tho' it seems very slow to the eye.

October, 1963

Returning to teaching was stressful for me, but I gradually adjusted to it, and Dora adjusted to daytime care at the babysitter's house. When our house was ready in May, we moved our pieces of furniture into a few rooms of our large, new house. The remainder of the house would need yet to be furnished.

At least I had the summer months to look forward to before Clyde and Laura arrived in September. There was time to enjoy Dora now and also time for marital intimacy. However, I was having trouble with responding, perhaps because of the anxiety of the past year or perhaps because at age twenty-seven I had gone through a sudden change of life. I remember the day after my hysterectomy. My breasts had suddenly hardened into painful stones. When the doctor came in for his daily visit, he explained that the sudden loss of the ovaries had produced a hormonal change, against which my body was rebelling. He dealt with it by shots of hormones and then prescribed estrogen suppositories. Still, my vagina had remained unhealthy and slow to respond to sex.

Will was unhappy about this, but instead of discussing it with me, he confided in a female coworker, a French-Canadian married woman, who was obviously experienced. She commiserated with him, and then after learning more about him, she suggested that some women were innately cold and needed professional help from a sexologist. When Will came home, he told me about their conversation and suggested that *I*, not *we*, should get professional help. I felt betrayed, unloved, misunderstood, and angry. I chided him for revealing intimate information between husband and wife. Will would not admit to his wrongdoing—a pattern with him.

I was not surprised when he lost his job six months later when this coworker turned against him.

In reviewing this period of our marital life, I realized that Will had forgotten the pain, suffering, and fear of death that I had gone through just a year prior. We had no assurance that I would remain free of cancer until the next four years had passed, and he had committed us to this new responsibility with his parents. After his death, I understood better that he had seen himself, not me, as the brave victim during that stressful time. He wrote in one of his autobiographical remembrances:

> *The transfusions were continuing, but Beth suddenly started to scream in pain. I saw her hospital physician going by and called him to attend to my wife. He summed up the situation immediately, went to the nurses' station and finding no one there (!) mustered me into service. Grabbing a load of towels, he told me to keep handing him the towels as he soaked up the blood resulting from his pressing repeatedly on her abdomen. Pretty soon the doorway to her room was crowded with nurses. The doctor*

rounded on them that they had vacated the nurses' station and told them to "Get the hell out—her husband is doing a fine job." The immediacy of the situation is what kept me going, but finally, when he was finished, I had to sit down to avoid fainting.

Also, I had a better understanding of Laura's need to be close to her medically vulnerable son. Will's autobiographical sketch, "Will at Deacon's School," portrays what life had been like for Will and his family during the war years of 1942 and 1943—

My parents enrolled me early in Deacon's. I was nine, turning ten in October. Shortly after starting school I fell off my bike and broke my right arm. I had a compound fracture. After six weeks, the plaster was removed and the arm had bent into a bulge. The doctors were going to leave it at that, but my maternal grandfather, who had accompanied me to the de-plastering, was adamantly not having that. "You're not going to leave this young boy with a dis-figured arm! Do something about it!" So the arm was re-broken and re-set. This time after another six weeks, the arm was as good as new.

With an arm in plaster, it was almost impossible to write with my right hand. This enabled me to avoid having to take any written tests, that is, until the teacher found out that I had taught myself to write quite adequately with my left hand. With a smile, she told me I would get to go back and take all the tests. (So I was found out and suffered the consequences.)

There was one drawback to having a plastered arm. This was, if you needed to prepare to defecate in a hurry, due to an overwhelming need. The problem was getting all the buttons undone in time. (Yes, there were buttons in those days, not zippers.) So, on one occasion my mother came along on her bicycle and found me striding along with a stick over my shoulder attached to a wrapped ball of soiled underpants.

"What on earth is that?" she said, "You look like a regular hobo!" I told her what I had in the bag and that I was bringing the underpants home to be washed. Clothes, like many other things, were strictly rationed during the war.

In the early spring of 1943, I became very sick. I already had a "heart murmur" from my mother having contracted scarlet fever before I was born. In March I was diagnosed with a combination of illnesses: rheumatic fever, meningitis, pneumonia, appendicitis, and jaundice. I was completely comatose, received a lumbar puncture for the meningitis, and was not expected to live. When I miraculously recovered, I awoke to find a Master Sergeant from South Carolina at my bedside. My family had befriended him at church.

I greeted him, "Sir, you're the first Yankee I've ever met."

"I ain't no goddam Yankee," he responded. He forgave me for my ignorance and continued to visit me regularly, even sending to the U.S. for a soccer ball, which turned out to be a water-polo ball!

What with the broken arm and the meningitis, I was technically in school for not quite half of the year. Even though I had passed the exams and was qualified to go into the next grade, my dear mother insisted I repeat the grade. This was embarrassing since there were several boys who were forced to repeat the grade, and I was lumped with these by a sarcastic teacher. I had been a grade ahead for my age when I entered the school, but to a boy my age, it was mortifying.

Although Will's doctor had warned Laura and Clyde that their son probably would not live long past "double figures," they kept him at the expensive Deacon's School for Boys. Before his death, Will was still proud to have been a Deaconian and had copied the Deaconian Crest and its Latin motto with its English translation onto his computer. The motto is in four parts:

"Quid quid agas prudenter agas"—"Whatever you do, do it well."

"Opulentiam aeternam gloriamque te promitto"—"Eternal riches and glory I promise thee."

"Quid quid agis prodenter a gas et respice finem"—"Whatever decision you choose to make, make sure to think about the consequences first."

"Venustatem infinitam gloriamque te promitto"—"Everlasting beauty and glory I promise thee."

Will had had years to think about the ill-fated plan that he and his mother had devised, but he had never taken responsibility for its consequences to our marriage.

Chapter 5

An Impossible Plan

Whoven Clyde and Laura arrived in September, 1964, Will and I turned over to them the care of Dora, the house, and the garden. Clyde became deeply unhappy within a few days. Unlike quiet, peaceful England with its few automobiles, he could neither bicycle nor walk into town, to church, to the "greengrocer's" or to the park. Although he had enjoyed gardening on his own small plot of land, he was chagrined by our one-acre plot landscaped with plants with which he was unfamiliar and that he disliked.

Clyde became depressed, but Laura became a tyrant. In England, among her relatives, she had been nicknamed "Lady Laura." Before we were married, Will had proudly called her that too. She had been the oldest in a family of eight girls. Early in life, she had determined to become better than they. She managed to get a better general education and to develop musical skills by taking voice lessons. (Will was proud of her beautiful contralto voice and her acting skills portrayed in her roles in local operettas.) She had also taken lessons in French and English speech and had developed an upper-class accent, unlike the local Peterborough accent of her sisters. Finally, she did not want to be simply a housewife, so she had gone to business school to learn bookkeeping. During marriage she had been not only the bookkeeper but often the manager of a local floral shop when the owner was involved with civic affairs.

She had raised her son to be like her. Will had been sent to Deacon's; he had been given private voice and violin lessons and had been encouraged to publicly perform. He had received French lessons from a tutor and private lessons in public speaking. She had told him that she was preparing him to be able to go anywhere and mingle with anyone. She had prepared him for university, and he had succeeded in becoming the first college graduate in his family. Unfortunately, she had not expected him to move to Canada. He should have married an upper-class girl and become a successful mathematician in England. Laura had laid a guilt trip on him about leaving home after all she had done for him. Furthermore, he had married an American who had come from humble farming ancestors. Now Laura was expected to become my housekeeper, maid, and babysitter. How humiliating it was for her!

Will was foolish not to realize that he was putting both his mother and his wife in an impossible situation. I learned from Clyde's memoirs that Laura had had a history of psychological problems: *She had a spell in the Chelsea Hospital for Women. Several times in the Middlesex, once in Guys, and was an inmate at Papworth.* What was Will thinking of, subjecting his young wife and two-year-old child to an unstable, perhaps explosive, situation?

It was not long before the explosion took place. Will and I came home one Friday afternoon to find Laura in a rage. She had taken a message from the adoption agency that we had consulted before the plan by Will and Laura had been hatched. Directing her words at me, she yelled, "So you expect me to take care of someone else's God-damned brat in addition to yours!" I said nothing as Will gathered Dora and told me to take her out.

When I returned with Dora hours later, Will relayed to me the dramatic story of what had happened: Laura attacked him on the stairs, trying to push him into a fall. He had wrestled with her and finally subdued her. She went to her bedroom, locked the door, and took an overdose of her sleeping tablets. Authorities had been called, had handcuffed her and taken her to a hospital for the weekend. Clyde had stood by throughout, wringing his hands and mumbling.

Laura was released from the hospital on Sunday evening with an appointment for a family meeting with a psychiatrist. It did not take the doctor long to analyze the situation. Laura directed most of her venom at me, accusing me of subjecting her to a filthy disease when she did my underwear in the laundry—looking for and finding a discharge from the estrogen suppositories. I had no need to explain to the doctor, who knew my medical history. His advice to Laura and Clyde was to go back to England—happy words for Clyde but useless for Laura.

When we returned home, she informed us that she had no intention of returning to England. Will called my parents and asked them to fly from Nebraska to help him convince Laura of her need to return. After a lengthy conversation my father had with her at our home, we felt that he had convinced her to come to her senses. My parents stayed a few days and helped them to pack. We all drove to the airport together, Mom and Dad leaving first on a plane to Nebraska. After my parents had left, Laura said, "Good! Now we don't have to go back." Clyde was terrified. When Will threatened to commit her again, she knew that she had lost the battle and joined Clyde on their flight to England.

Will never apologized to me for his mother's behavior. He was a victim, in no way responsible for the failure of the plan. In his autobiographical description of the story, he became the hero, Laura was the villain, and I was a minor character. I am reminded of lines in his poem to Gisela, which was good advice if he had applied it to himself:

Let her note that you have
A central purpose in life,
And such a purpose
That will not exclude her,
But rather that she may enter into
And help promote.
She is to be your helpmate
And so do not frustrate her
By non-inclusion in your schemes.

January, 1959

I wondered if he would have included Gisela in his plan if he had married her instead of me.

In Clyde's memoirs, he described this time as "harrowing." Their return home was embarrassing for both of them. Clyde relayed how they needed to explain to people "over and over again" until he got "thoroughly fed up with it." Clyde never blamed me for the tragedy, but to Laura, I remained the "ugly American."

Although Clyde had disliked the American culture, Laura disliked much more about the Americans: She resented the USA for succeeding the British Empire as a major power in the world. She thought it unfair that the U.S. had entered World War I so late, allowing England to shoulder the burden of the war. When World War II began, the U.S. had again waited until England was on the verge of destruction before the "Yanks" had joined the battle. After the war, England was left destitute while the U.S. had become wealthier and had chosen to help the country of Germany to rebuild rather than helping their ally, Britain.

She preferred the English system of education, which was geared to a distinction between those capable of only a general education and those intelligent enough to be admitted to the private system of the upper classes. The Americans were too egalitarian, trying to educate everyone.

America lacked the majesty and beauty of the former empire, which still existed in its palaces, stately homes, cathedrals, royalty, pomp and circumstance, the Houses of Parliament and other great institutions of law and education, formal English gardens, and an ancient code of chivalry.

She resented wealthy Americans who came to England to experience all these things while demanding their three-minute boiled eggs, cold beer, iced water, and fresh salads. They wanted a private bath adjoining their hotel room. They wanted the restaurants and pubs to be open whenever they felt like eating or drinking. They valued money and what money could purchase, such as English antiques instead of culture. But they refused to learn the English system of coinage with its pounds, shillings, and pennies, not easily converted to the decimal system of the U.S.

She disliked what the Americans had done to the English language. They had substituted words such as "while" for "whilst," "two weeks" for "fortnight," "garbage can" for "dustbin," "bar" for "pub." She hated the lazy, unclipped accent of the Americans, slurring the word "water" into "wad-der" instead of "wah-tuh."

Will remained in some ways an English "snob" from March, 1964, when he received his certificate of naturalization in the U.S., until he died in 2018. On the computer, he made long lists of American replacements of English words. He refused to use the American replacements of some of these throughout his life. When it was to his advantage, he loved emphasizing his English accent. Most of the anglophiles I knew admired Will's accent and the English ways he chose to keep, making him often the center of attention.

In 1961 he wrote a poem called "English" that reveals the superiority he felt for the language and its history:

English is the tongue which
Calmly, and without too much
Fervor, allows expression
Of the deepest thoughts of man.

The romantic power of the
Romance vernaculars is undenied;
Also the precise and staccato
Majesty of the Teuton tongue is evident.

But there is a splendor in English:
There is the capacity for great beauty.

English, skillfully used,
Is a language of simplicity,
Of easy, pithy renderings
Of the mind's images,
Of the soul's yearnings and desires.
     English is the language of poetry.

Chapter 6

WILL, BETH, AND DORA

From October 1964 until November 1967, Will, Dora, and I led a happy family life. Will was working at his fourth job since coming to California. With his education and his innate talents, this was probably the best job he had had to date. Litton-Mellonics, a subcontractor through Aerospace Corporation, was supplying the U.S. government with Satellite Command and Control programs. Will's job was to use his mathematical skills to study existing code for computers (which at that time were slow and had little memory) and find number conversions to reduce time-costly looping. He became a hero at Mellonics when he wrote his "Bin, Fill & Spill" program, which reduced the loading time for the code by 67 %, making it possible for the U.S. to install a new antenna for a satellite.

I, too, now healthier and more energetic, was enjoying more my work as an English teacher. My life was unbelievably busy. Three of my female friends from the English Department, their husbands, and Will and I met on Saturday evenings for a dinner at one of our houses. When it was my turn to be hostess, my week followed a typical pattern: school during the weekdays, grading papers Monday through Thursday evenings, dinner out with Will and Dora on Friday evenings, up early on Saturdays to clean house and prepare dinner for eight. Will helped me to entertain our guests and then clean up after the party. On Sundays we attended church in the morning. Afternoons were naptime for Dora and a time for marital intimacy for Will and me. After her nap, Dora always climbed into bed with us so that we could play "Patty-cake" and "Five Little Piggies" with her.

On the weeknights when I was busy with school-work, Will escorted Dora to bed. Each night he stayed with her at her bedside and sang songs to her, such as "The Owl and the Pussycat," helped her with her prayers, and tucked her in. This routine led to a close relationship between them, one that has remained.

His darling poem titled "Mr. Bear" is about the English teddy-bear sent to Dora by Clyde and Laura.

Dora both loved and mistreated Mr. Bear throughout her childhood.

This is the tale of Mr. Bear,
Whose sad, sad fate was less than fair.

OBSERVER: *"Mr. Bear, Mr. Bear,*
    What on earth are you doing down there?"

MR. BEAR: *"It's a sad, sad tale I have to tell—*
    How out of bed I tumbled and fell.
        I didn't really fall at all:
        I was rudely thrown, as I recall;
    My little mistress got hold of my arm,
    (She didn't know she was doing me harm),
        And swung me around and threw me out,
        (I hit the ground with quite a clout),
    I'm lying down here wondering when
    I'll have the good fortune to be lifted again
        To a position from which I can look around
        —Instead of lying face down on the ground;
    But I know the sad fate that's bound to be—
    To be thrown around almost constantly."

During this period of Dora's youth, Will on special occasions became the "poetical Santa Claus" and the "poetical tooth fairy." In preparation for Christmas Eve, Will and I joined together to find hiding places where Santa could leave his gifts. Then Will wrote a poem for each one, giving Dora clues for finding it. The following is from Christmas Eve, 1965:

> *This year, sweet Dora, Santa brings*
> *Four pretty packaged play-time things.*
> > *The first, though not so scary,*
> > *Is really rather hairy.*
> *You'll find it in a sink,*
> *I think.*
> > *The second is the Shepherd's cry!*
> > *"Early morning, sky so red,"*
> > > *"Oh My!"*
> > *You'll find it in a drawer,*
> > *What's more!*
> *The third is awfully like the last;*
> *But now the sky is blue (not overcast).*
> *You'll find it under bed of sleepy head.*
> *(Don't wake him).*
> > *The fourth is made of finest cloth*
> > *(The kind to guard against the moth).*

This one is in a kitchen closet;
That wasn't hard at all—
Or was it?
There are times you're not as good
As you should be;
But those times are rather rare
And Santa's fair.
He knows many girls much worse
Who strut and kick and curse.
So be better still my pretty lass
And please remember not to "Sass."
Grow straight and slim and kind and true,
Then there's nothing in the world
Too good for you.

By age six, Dora had figured out the game, and she had begun to write to Santa or to the tooth fairy. When she had lost her sixth tooth, she left the tooth and a childish note for the fairy under her pillow. Fortunately, the tooth fairy found it when she was asleep and responded by taking the tooth and replacing her note with his poem:

To the dear, dear girl who writes
Such nice notes to the Tooth-Fairy—
The last little girl who wrote so well to me
Was called Mary
      —or was it Carrie?
Before your tooth I had collected five
Trillion teeth.
Thanks so much for the sixth—
The special one—
Now I have five trillion-six.

The last tooth was from a young
Fellow called Heath—
      —or was it Keith?
I'm so very forgetful—
      I sometimes forget to show up—
Especially when my little friends
Start to grow up—

Go show off, here's a buck
And lots of luck—
Go have yourself lots of fun.

By Dora's birthday in 1967, Will's former "skiing lifestyle" had caught up with him. His aortic valve had calcified to the point where there was little room for the blood to pass through. Open-heart surgery was still rare and not easily performed by surgeons, but Will had no choice if he wanted to extend his life. Surgery was scheduled for December, whenever a human valve (a homograft) became available.

We were both extremely worried. I was facing the likelihood of becoming a widow at age thirty-two with a six-year-old child to raise. Will was facing death and the day-to-day difficulty of keeping his job as his energy decreased.

Our marital intimacy suddenly ceased. Will plopped into bed one night, quickly masturbated, turned over with his back to me, and immediately fell asleep. I lay there, flabbergasted. I felt a combination of anxiety for him, embarrassment for me, and sorrow for us. Unfortunately, after the surgery, when he had again regained his health, this method of "self-love" too often replaced intimacy with me. For him, it was quicker, easier, and required much less effort. I always felt rejected, lonely, and unloved.

The open-heart surgery and the recuperation following were like the differences between crawling and walking in comparison to surgery and recovery today. Since Will's blood type was O-negative, he needed to recruit coworkers to donate the twenty pints of blood that were needed for surgery at that time. They gladly did this, making him again the center of attention at the office. None of them had known anyone who had gone through the bravery of having his heart stopped, operated on, and restarted again. One of the artists in the group drew a caricature of Will, and each of his coworkers signed it and sent it home with him on his last day before surgery.

The day of the surgery I sat in the waiting room from early morning until mid-afternoon. To keep my mind from worry, I marked up a stack of compositions. Because the surgery lasted so long, fluid had built up in Will's lungs. He had to overcome pneumonia as well as the reknitting of bone and tissue as he recuperated. After a long stay in the hospital, he was allowed to complete his healing at home. For the next month, he experienced difficulty breathing at night. After a long day of work, I frequently needed to bundle up Dora and carry her to the car for a 2:00 or 3:00 AM trip to the hospital to get help for Will.

By the summer of 1968, I was the one who needed to recuperate. However, it was a delightful summer with

Dora—watching her learn to swim, playing with her in the sand at the beach, enjoying her playing "teacher" with the children in our cul-de-sac. The children were all similar in age, but I was the teacher on the block, and that made Dora the likely one to play that role.

When school began again in the fall, we were all ready for it and for work. Now a second-grader, Dora returned to the country private school we had chosen for her—a place to learn and to experience the joy of riding horses and playing soccer. After school or on Saturdays, I drove her to a ballet lesson or piano lesson. Later, she became proficient at the oboe. Unlike Will's upbringing, I insisted that Dora not be pressured to perform unless she was required to as a member of an orchestra or band.

In the summer of 1970, Will and I took Dora for a vacation to England to reintroduce her to her grandparents and to see the country of Will's birth. Enough time had passed since their disastrous stay with us. I too was looking forward to seeing Peterborough and learning about its history and culture. Will's stylized poem "The Nene" had given me a flavor of this area:

The Nene a jolie river is;
filled are her waters full of fish,
that many an angler's lyne and rod

hath landed strate upon the sod.

Medeshamstede* lieth on her bank,
which once beneath the Wash was sank;
a port it was of fayre renowne,
and latterly a busy towne;

a camp nearby the Romans made,
a ford across the river laid
at Castor where the Nene is shallow,
and the pastures lush and fallow.

*ancient name for Peterborough
written in Southampton, Autumn, 1955

Laura, who was the president of the local Bible Society, invited me to be the "Opener of the Summer Fayre" at the Town Hall. That meant my giving a speech. I chose the topic of English cathedrals, and I described my impressions of the cathedrals at Lincoln, Ely, York, and Peterborough.

Following the program, I was interviewed by a female reporter from the local newspaper. Midway in my discussion with her of an American's impressions of the cathedrals, the thatched cottages, and the beautiful green countryside I had bicycled through, Will rushed up, interrupted our conversation, and turned the attention to himself. He droned on and on about all the antique purchases we had made to furnish our large house in America—a Victorian velvet settee with matching his and hers chairs, a brass fender for the fireplace, a silver tea service, among others—and our plans to have them shipped around the tip of South America to a port in San Francisco.

Silently I stood by, realizing the impending consequences of his pride. Although I was not a celebrity, an article in the newspaper the following morning included a picture of me and the headline "American Antique Huntress in Peterborough." The vicious article described me as one of the wealthy Americans who were buying up all the English antiques.

A family gathering and dinner were held at the house of one of Will's relatives in the afternoon. Everybody had seen the article. No one mentioned it, but I was ostracized. I took a corner seat and stayed there while Will happily mingled with his aunts, uncles, cousins, and their spouses and children. Laura had witnessed the event of the reporter's interview and neither explained it to the group nor apologized to me. Will did not admit that he had misbehaved either to his relatives or to me, the "ugly American." Dora was too young to understand what had happened.

The purchase of the English antiques began a period of materialism for Will and me. Our big house gradually began to look more like a museum than a home. In addition to the English antiques, we purchased American antiques as well as Oriental carpets, oil paintings and watercolors, and pieces of antique chinaware. Church on Sundays was sometimes skipped for a weekend visit to galleries in San Francisco or Carmel. Pride replaced happiness.

We were headed in the wrong direction—not the direction of love for each other or spiritual love. Materialism left no room for gratitude: thankfulness for a life that had not been cut short; for science and the doctors who had been successful; for life in America, where open-heart surgery had been possible at this time; for friends and coworkers who had given of themselves; for a wife who had prayed for and stood by her husband during dark days and nights. It was as though Will had reverted to the self-gratification days of skiing in Colorado, and I was along for the ride. Will had expressed this ride well in a poem dating back to

January, 1960, when he was living in Whittier, CA, working at IBM, and skiing on the weekends.

Devil Drive
(Temptation)

He was in limbo,
Wrestling with the demon spirits from Hades
Who had it in their power to start their ter-
rible tortures
At the first sign of human weakness.
    Before his eyes, and into his mind
    Flowed images designed to tempt him:
    Beautiful-bodied vamps beckoned him,
    Cavorting in a lascivious cabaret;
Girls like these he had lusted after on earth,
But here in limbo, he was without interest.
Sensuous, undulating forms now failed to move him;
Failed to stir the consuming passions he had
known before.
    He looked, not with complete indifference,
    But yet he was acquiring the immortal's
    Imperviousness to carnal things;
Even when the demons produced magnifi-
cent spreads

Of exotic food, he was not to be swayed.
He seemed aware that an immortal has
No need for even the necessities of the flesh.
   The arch-demon had a new idea!
   He and his hordes set to
   To fabricate a wondrous thing:
   A transcendentalised racing automobile!
When they had finished their creation
They beckoned their prey anew,
With smirks of satanic savvy on their faces,
Yes! He had to get in!
He had to get behind the wheel and drive this machine!
   Once in, he closed the door,
   Positioned the seat, adjusted the mirrors,
   Turned on the ignition, and pressed the gas-pedal.
As the machine accelerated, he realized
He could not control it. He could not escape;
He found himself hurtling through the gaping jaws of Hell,
Found himself met by the hosts of darkness,
Lustily chanting their refrain:
   Tried for lust;
   Lust and pride;

Pride and lust;
Trussed and tied.
The devils congratulated Satan
That he had so cunningly contrived
And won the very soul of this and future Americans;
And Satan, in his own demonic heart,
Acknowledged the world's automobile designers
For giving the victim his preconditioned response.
He made a mental note to include them
In his latest "Who's Who in Hell!"

Chapter 7

CHANGES

~~~~~•~~~~~

*N*ot long after we returned from our trip to England, Will moved from Mellonics to Fairchild Systems in Palo Alto, to a position where he would be a programmer and manager of a small group of systems analysts. When he turned thirty-nine in October, he reached the age when many males begin going through a midlife crisis. Will was showing signs of this. Much of his discussion at home about his new job seemed to be centered on a coworker named Victoria, whom he consistently described as "brilliant."

The company held its annual dinner dance in the early spring—an elegant affair requiring the women to wear evening gowns and the men to be formally attired. For the occasion, I had purchased a lovely gown at I. Magnin in San Francisco. It was a white silk gown with a matching silk shawl. A purple flower and green-leaf Oriental-looking design spread along the bottom of the skirt. The white silk was embroidered with geometric elongated circles made of golden threads. It was fitted to the waist and then flowed freely but slimly from the waist down. My figure, still 34-24-34, was perfect for the dress.

When I dressed for the evening of the dinner dance and presented myself to Will, I expected to receive a "Wow!" Instead, his response was, "Very nice." At the ballroom, the party was divided into circular tables of eight. Will and I sat with the men he managed at work and their wives or girlfriends. Will dominated the conversation, leaving me to be one of the listeners. Much of the conversation was about one of the vice presidents, Elton E— — —, who had just left the company after undergoing several sex-change operations. A good-looking man in his forties, he had opened a transvestite bar in San Francisco. He had left his wife and three children and a successful job for a complete lifestyle change. He and Will had exchanged poetry while Elton was still with Fairchild; perhaps the clue to Elton's future had been in the eroticism and fantasy found within the poems. After reading one of the poems, I advised Will to return the collection unread.

Although couples at our table were dancing, Will did not ask me to dance. When I returned from a trip to the ladies' room, Will was dancing with Victoria. I watched as he escorted her back to her table and then took a seat next to her to continue their conversation. Returning to our table, he said, "Let's go." That was it—the end of an evening of sitting like a mannequin in a beautiful dress.

In the spring of 1971, a bad car accident changed the direction we had been going. Will, Dora, and I had met for dinner one evening at a restaurant. Afterward, Will turned right in his car onto a busy street, and Dora and I turned left in my car. A truck driven by a drunkard came barreling through the red light and hit my car broadside, with the point of impact directly on my door. Will witnessed the accident in his rearview mirror and came running. Dora had been playing on the floor in the rear of the car and was thrown onto the back seat. She suffered only minor injuries.

I had seen the truck coming at a high speed, and I knew that this was the end for me, and perhaps Dora as well. At the impact, my heavy old Oldsmobile refused to overturn, but it spun around and around, each time my head hitting the metal side of the door. When I miraculously was released from the car, my head was swollen to twice its size. X-rays at the hospital showed no broken bones, but I was kept there until most of the fluid inside my skull had been released. One orange-sized lump above my left eye took four months to be absorbed.

The remainder of the spring and throughout the summer, I recuperated at home. A period of anxiety and depression set in. For three months, I had weekly sessions with a psychiatrist, first for the anxiety and then to discuss my experiences and feelings that had led to my unhappiness at age thirty-six. Although I was too embarrassed to explain fully my marital intimate times with Will, both Dr. S. and I realized that this was a significant reason for my unhappiness. Dr. S. continued to encourage Will to have a session of analysis with him.

Finally, Will agreed to meet with the doctor privately. On our way home from Will's meeting, which had followed my session, he reported that Dr. S. had found no need for another session with him — Will was well-adjusted! It was obvious to me that Will had not been forthright about his background or our present life. At ages thirty-six and thirty-nine, we could still have developed a beautiful, loving relationship if both of us had been open and honest.

When I returned to school in the fall, I had been assigned two new classes and a room at the back of the gymnasium, which had no windows but plenty of noise from bouncing basketballs throughout the day. By the end of the semester, I could no longer endure the glare of harsh electric lights, the noise, and the feeling that I was working primarily to maintain a large, richly decorated house without love. I resigned from public school teaching at the beginning of the new semester.

Will was not prepared for me to be just a homemaker. Perhaps he was worried about being the sole wage earner, and he didn't like the prospect of strictly budgeting; or perhaps he was comparing me with Laura, who had worked outside the home her entire life. I needed a rest, but I was not allowed to have one.

Will soon found me a teaching position in the computer industry. I had just a month to take classes to learn the PDP-8 and then develop lesson plans to teach a weeklong class for adult students whose companies had purchased this new, small computer. The course included training in the classroom and in the computer lab. It was a daunting task for an ex–English teacher. Will was working nearby in another company, but he came only twice to have lunch with me. He preferred to play bridge with coworkers at lunchtime. On the whole,

I was left to "sink or swim" on my own. My students wrote good critiques of my teaching skills, but my manager felt that I was not advancing quickly enough. By the end of six months, I was unemployed.

Meanwhile, Will had become discontented with Fairchild and had decided, together with a group of programmers, to found their own company. They would each put in capital equivalent to the position they would have in the company. Will wanted to be the chief scientist, and he would have enough capital if we remortgaged our house in Saratoga. With my PDP-8 teaching job still so new, I encouraged him to wait for another opportunity to become an entrepreneur.

However, Will was a risk-taker. He had shown this in the past when he had left his secure job in Canada for the dangerous ski slopes of Colorado. His poem "Nil Carborundum," a rhyming acrostic sonnet, shows him to have been a seeker of dreams, oblivious of the cost:

N   *"Nil Carborundum" was the merry cry:*
I   *"In very truth"—the damsel gave reply—*
L   *"Lift not your hands to tasks too strong for them:*

C   *Clean hands and hearts are the purest emblem,*

A   *And no virtue lies in flogging horses—*
R   *(Rivers should not wander from their courses,*
B   *But rather they should be quite regular)."*
O   *Oft-times I've heard these cries from way afar,*
R   *Resounding   through   my   head   and*
       through my soul:
U   *"Unless you watch out you will miss your goal—*
N   *Never will you have the chance to return—*
D   *Do what you will with haste before you burn:"*
U   *Useless to squirm and hope to dodge the cost,*
M   *Meaningless the fight when your soul is lost.*

nil = Latin word meaning "nothing"
carborundum = a compound of carbon and silicon used in polishing

I, "the damsel," could not convince Will of the virtue of playing it safe for the sake of our family. He took out a large mortgage on our house (in eight years it had doubled in value), and we engaged in the struggle for the new company to succeed. Like most new venture projects, it failed for lack of funds within six months.

Since Will had no scientific problems to solve at the company, he created intellectual puzzles at home, either a mathematical problem to solve or a homemade device that could be taken apart and reassembled. Our closets were filled with these, with which he played and enticed others to try to solve. One of these puzzles he called Hi-IQubes, for which he wrote a twenty-one-page manual, with three pages of illustrations and eighteen pages of explanation. It was designed for players of only MENSA IQ. (Will had taken the admission test for the American MENSA organization and had scored at or above the 98th percentile needed to become a member.) He did not join this exclusive club, but the test had probably given him ideas for his puzzle. Will hired a patent attorney, who tried to obtain a patent for Hi-IQubes, but the puzzle remained an unfulfilled dream. Perhaps if Will had aimed his puzzle at players with less than 160 IQ, his chances of success would have been greater.

When my job failed, we needed to solve our financial problems: a bigger mortgage and no income. We sold our large house in Saratoga at twice its original cost and moved to a much smaller house in Los Gatos, one that was in need of repairs and improvement.

Since we were both temporarily unemployed, we worked together to lay a brick patio at the back of the house and slate on the walkway and porch in front. We also tiled the entryway, the kitchen and bath counters, and the fireplace ledges. After Will had started a new job as an applications programmer at Atallah/Tandem, I continued remodeling our home by refinishing wood-work and repainting walls. Then I landscaped the front and rear gardens. All of this manual labor left both of us with a feeling of achievement and satisfaction in working together.

Dora had one more year at the private school before we sent her to public junior high. For a few years, I enjoyed my time as a homemaker and gardener while simultaneously becoming a student again. By taking courses in math at the local junior college, I felt that I could converse somewhat with Will about one of his areas of expertise. Occasional questions I asked him about homework, however, must have made me appear naïve. He impatiently helped me. However, when Dora was beginning her sophomore year in high school, I used the math courses to my advantage. Louise, a teacher friend of mine, had informed me that the private school Dora had attended was looking for a math and algebra teacher for their seventh- and eighth-graders.

The school year was about to begin, and the principal was anxious to fill the position.

We had a brief interview. From my résumé he saw that I had a BS in Education from the University of Nebraska, an MEd from the University of Arizona, fifteen years of teaching experience, and a California lifetime secondary credential. Although English and music had been my subject fields, I was termed qualified to teach any subject in grades seven through twelve. Having recently reviewed high school math and done well in junior college math classes, I felt confident in accepting a teaching role in math and algebra for grades seven and eight. During the interview, the principal had primarily talked about himself rather than asking me questions about myself.

I accepted the position, but I knew that I would be answering to an intellectual snob in a "country school." Mr. R. had come from a wealthy family, had attended an Eastern prep school before an Ivy League college, and had given himself the title of headmaster of the school. In spite of his pretentious attitude, I enjoyed my work and did well, getting good year-end reviews.

During the second semester of my third year, I needed a substitute for a week because I was having surgery. Mr. R. came to our home for materials and plans that I had left with Will. That was the beginning of the end of my teaching career.

Will invited Mr. R. in and immediately began talking about himself: his degree in Pure Math from the University of London, his tutoring me in math in junior college, and his helping me with the algebra class I was now teaching. (Only once or twice had I needed help.) Headmaster R. was aghast! He had hired a teacher who didn't know her subject field!

When I returned to school, I sensed his coolness but didn't know then why his attitude had changed. Two weeks before the end of the school year, I had not had an annual review. I understood why when Headmaster R. came to my classroom at the end of the day on a Friday and told me that he was terminating me after the final day of the year—two weeks' notice. The reason that he gave was that I was not the kind of teacher he wanted on his staff.

Feeling that this was the end of my teaching career, I angrily responded, "If I am such a poor teacher, I wouldn't want you to put up with me for the next two weeks. I'm leaving now, not in two weeks."

"You can't do that!" he shouted. "Final grades are due!"

"Here's my grade book. You figure them out." I collected my things and walked out of the door. During the next two weeks, I had calls from board members and parents wanting an explanation. If Will answered the phone, he explained it from his point of view, and I realized that his self-centeredness had contributed to my failure.

Chapter 8

SEARCHING FOR HAPPINESS

During the last two years, while still teaching, I had accepted a part-time position as organist at a nearby Episcopal church. Having played piano since age five, I was a skilled pianist, and I had an innate talent for music. When Mr. J. left his position as organist, the rector encouraged me to work into the position. He was willing to let me temporarily use just the manuals of the organ until I could become proficient with the pedal board. I knew enough about the difference between a piano and an organ to realize that this would be a time-consuming task, but when I left teaching, I suddenly had all week to practice for a Sunday service.

I began taking organ lessons and found that playing the organ required coordination of hands, arms, feet, and legs; building up new muscles; changing posture; learning different fingering and finger-sub-stitution techniques; applying a smooth, legato touch instead of a percussive one; and reading music in a unique way. Unlike piano music, which is read with the mind assigning the treble clef to the right hand and the bass clef to the left, organ music is more complicated. For example, to read hymns for the organ, the mind must separate the music into three divisions, with the right hand playing the treble staff, the left hand playing the tenor part of the bass staff, and the feet playing the bass part on the pedal board. Solo organ music and scores for accompaniment are often written with three or more staves, requiring a simultaneous vertical/hor-izontal reading of the music. At age forty-one, I was learning to rethink thirty-six years of piano music while developing new physical skills for playing organ music.

I spent many hours practicing at church to learn these skills and to prepare for Sunday services, wed-dings and funerals, and anthem accompaniment for choir or vocal solos. Gradually, a male member of the church staff, seeing me daily, developed an interest in me. I was flattered at first but then became concerned that my marriage would be compromised when his advances became bolder. When I relayed this to Will and asked him to speak with my "admirer" or with the rector, he ignored my request. I wondered if Will was even a bit jealous.

One summer evening I found out. Will had invited Tom, a coworker, and his wife for dinner at our home. It was a very hot night. We had all had too many Planter's Punch after-dinner cocktails. Tom suggested that we all enjoy the swimming pool. Will, unable to swim, and Tom's wife sat at the edge of the pool while Tom, in his boxer shorts, and I, in my bra and panties, stepped into the pool. The night was dark, no lights were on, and Tom and I were enjoying the cool water. Tom removed his shorts for a "skinny-dip" and I joined him in a playful but harmless hour of fun in the pool. After the couple had left, I expected Will to discuss the incident with me, but he did not mention it. He showed no jealousy or concern during that evening or afterward.

Dora, now in her senior year at high school, had fallen in love with a handsome young boy named Vince. They had an obvious electric attraction to each other, mental and physical. Will was concerned, but I reminded him that she had had sex education at high school and girlfriends who had discussed the subject. I did not feel the need for parental advice. However, Will did. He entered Dora's bedroom one evening directly after she had gone to bed and sat down at her bedside as he had done during her early childhood; instead of singing "The Owl and the Pussycat," he explained to her how to release sexual desire by "self-love." (Will always lacked sensitivity for another's feelings.)

Vince had invited Dora to the prom. In preparation for the event, Will and I took them out for hamburgers and a discussion. We all enjoyed the conversation; they were looking forward to the prom, and we were enjoying their anticipation of the event. After lunch, Vince and Dora drove off in Vince's car, and Will and I headed for home in ours. I talked about Vince's handsome appearance and his wit, Will about Dora's beauty. I suddenly said to him, "As the mother of a beauty, at what percentile would you put me for women?" Without hesitation, he answered, "Fiftieth percentile."

I had never been a vain female. My mother had made sure of that, but I had always considered myself above average in appearance. In my heart, I knew that his quick response had not been made in jest. Instead, it confirmed the actions he displayed when he flirted with other women in my presence, letting me know that he found them more attractive.

Dora had begun developing into a beauty when she was almost fourteen. Will had secretly had a two-and-a-half-by-four-foot portrait painted of her, inviting my friend Louise to participate in the secrecy while the portrait was being painted at her home and later in a surprise fortieth birthday party for me. The evening of my birthday, Will took me for a ride. When we returned home, the portrait had been prominently displayed on a mahogany easel placed behind the lower section of the Victorian settee. I pretended to be pleased. I had never hinted at wanting a portrait of Dora. I knew that it was not so much for me as it was for him.

From Dora's childhood until close to the time of his death, Will had addressed her as "Beautiful" or "Darling" or "Sweetie" or even "Lover." Except for the early days of our marriage, I was most often "Beth" and occasionally "Honey." However, more upsetting to me was how he described other women as "attractive" or "brilliant."

In the fall of 1978, Will took a trip alone to be with his father, who had broken his femur. From Clyde's memoir, I later learned that Laura had been in the Middlesex Hospital for psychological treatment during that time. Will suddenly extended his two-week trip to England with a trip to Wiesbaden, Germany, where he stayed in the apartment of a young bachelor named Kurt, whom Will had never mentioned. When Will returned home, he had numerous photos of Wiesbaden and stories of the fun that Kurt and he had had attending folk music festivals, wine tastings, and a boat excursion down the Rhine.

As a software consultant, Will frequently made trips within the U.S. to locations where he was sent by his company: El Paso, San Antonio, New Orleans, Boston, and New York City among them. He seldom called when away, but he always came back with stories of good times he had had. After each trip, Will returned with increased libido. A pattern of consequences followed: marital intimacy, vaginal infection, a visit to the doctor, testing, and antibiotic drugs. Eventually our internist suggested that the reoccurrence of chlamydia could be the result of Will's being the carrier. Fearing for his own health, Will allowed himself to be tested, was proven the carrier, and took the needed antibiotic drugs. When I discussed the issue with Will, he blamed his mother, Laura, for not having had him circumcised as a baby. He solved the problem of my vaginal infections by no further intimacy with me. I was forty-four; he was forty-seven.

As soon as Dora left for college in the fall of 1979, Will moved from the master bedroom to occupy the guest bedroom at night.

In 1980 Will's parents visited us in Los Gatos. Dora had spent a month with them in England in the summer of 1977, but I had not seen them since 1970, when I had been ostracized by the family. In spite of that incident, I was determined to be a hospitable American. While they were with us, Will and I hosted a fiftieth wedding anniversary party for them at our home. Clyde later described it in his memoir:

They gave us a right royal time. A reception was held around the swimming pool, and we were able to meet all their friends. Beth went out and bought card tables and chairs just for the occasion . . .

I had done most of the planning, decoration, and work for the party. During their stay with us, they did not see the true relationship between Will and me. We devoted our master bedroom and bath to them to comfortably and privately enjoy. Will and I took the bedroom with twin single beds, and Dora, who was home from college, reoccupied her bedroom. Will and I temporarily continued the sham of cohabitating. The separation resumed when Clyde and Laura left and Dora returned to college.

I made one more attempt at marital happiness by sessions with a woman psychologist, to whom I complained that I was treated like a piece of furniture in the house. She encouraged me to convince Will to have joint sessions, but he emphatically refused. As I look back on it, this was a turning point in our relationship. Unable to find happiness in love, I turned my hobby in music into a full-time career.

When I was trying out stops at an organ studio in San Francisco in the summer of 1979, a former student of Richard Purvis heard me play and suggested that I contact Mr. Purvis to see if he would accept me as a student. A retired organist and choirmaster at Grace Cathedral, he was still composing choral and organ music, giving concerts, and teaching organ lessons. After auditioning me, he accepted me as a student. At about the same time, I began studying for a BA and then an MA degree in music at San Jose State University. Since the university did not have an organ professor on board, they allowed me to be trained in organ performance by Mr. Purvis, and I began traveling to and from San Francisco for organ lessons.

Mr. Purvis encouraged me to seek a better church position so that I would have an adequate instrument for practicing and performance. I was soon employed by a large Lutheran church near the campus, first as an assistant and a year later as organist and director. The beautiful Schlicker pipe organ was a wonderful instrument for practice, for the worship services, and for the three concerts I was required to give for the degrees. In the first concert for a BA, I included several numbers for the bell choir that I had started and trained. Will was the only male ringer in the group. In the second concert, I included him to sing a chant-like solo I had composed for a composition class.

While I was busy with my music career, Will was a program manager at Ricoh, which had divisions in the U.S. and in Japan. Will had three Japanese programmers as trainees. From the first, there was a communication problem between them and Will. The three understood classroom English, but they had no idea of common American expressions. One day the three appeared in Will's office to ask him for the plans for the next phase of the program. Will, seated at his desk, arose and said, "I'm sorry. You've caught me with my pants down." The three immediately dropped their eyes to Will's ankles and Will burst into laughter.

Will tried to improve their communication skills by inviting them to our home for dinner and taking them on sightseeing outings, which he asked me to join in order to enable more conversation. The young Japanese men were always very polite to me and thanked me for my hospitality.

In the fall of 1984, Will was sent by Ricoh for a six-week business trip to Tokyo. He extended the trip by two weeks so that he could take his annual vacation in Japan. When I watched Will board the plane for Tokyo, he looked quite healthy. Unfortunately, the young Japanese programmers entertained him in *their* style, by following daytime work with evening pleasure—drinking, night-clubs, and public baths. Will called me one night around 3:00 AM my time. He was exuberant and so intoxicated I could barely understand his speech. I told him never to call me again in that state.

When I met him at the airport on his return, he looked debauched, like sixty-two instead of fifty-two. He was not physically ready to face 1985, which turned out to be a very stressful and eventful year for us.

In February, on the Saturday of Lincoln's Holiday, twenty-three years after Dora had been conceived during our ski trip to Squaw Valley, she married Vince, her first "heartthrob." It was a very large, expensive wedding and reception. The church was filled with local friends and parishioners and relatives from the East and the Midwest. I helped Dora with all the plans for the event, prepared the pre-wedding and wedding music, and devoted myself to the guests before, during, and after the event. Will photographed Dora in many poses at home even though we had a professional photographer for the occasion. Dora wore my beautiful taffeta gown and a lace veil of her choice. She looked gorgeous as she walked down the aisle with Will in a tuxedo.

The only sad point of the occasion for me was when the dancing began at the reception. Dora danced first with Vince and second with her dad. I sat watching, anticipating Will's dance with me. In my memory, I am still sitting there. Not once did we dance the entire evening.

We sent to England a tape of the ceremony, which included pre-wedding music by the bell choir and my playing "The Voluntary in D" by Purcell as the wedding march and the famous Widor "Toccata from Symphony No. 1" as the recessional. Clyde especially enjoyed and appreciated the tape.

Fortunately it arrived in Peterborough well before Laura's tragic fall. Although heavily dosed with sleeping tablets, Laura had awakened in the early morning and had headed down the steep stairs to get a glass of orange juice. Clyde wrote in his memoir:

> *I was awakened by a loud bang at 5:00*
> *A.M. on Thursday, the 12th of September.*
> *When I got to the stairs, the poor thing*
> *was at the foot of the stairs, with the side*
> *of her head smashed in. She tripped and*
> *tumbled down, smacking her head on*

a wooden hat stand at the bottom. She never regained consciousness. . . . The church was packed for the funeral service on 20th September. Will was not able to come over for the funeral. He was going into hospital for a replacement of a heart valve and a pacemaker.

Will's surgery was not until late December. Meanwhile, I gave my final organ concert for the MA and accompanied a trumpeter from England for two concerts in the area. The day of Will's surgery was also the day of my final written exam at the university. I rushed to the hospital afterward to see how Will was doing with his new homograft and pacemaker. I found him cheerfully sitting up in bed with an attractive nurse nearby. Will was never too ill to charm the nurses.

Many advances in heart surgery had been made within the last fifteen years, leading to less pain and quicker recovery for the patient. After a month of recuperation, Will was ready to return to work. However, instead of going back to the stress of Ricoh, he took a position as a scientific programmer in a pacemaker company.

Chapter 9

CROSSROADS

As a couple, we were at a crossroads. Will's mother had died, our daughter had married, and Will had a new job and a new homograft. I had completed my degrees in music, graduating summa cum laude, and was still young enough to work toward a PhD in music. I looked into the programs at Berkeley, where I could have commuted, and at the University of Arizona in Tucson, where I had gotten my MEd degree. The latter would have required my living away from home. I had been paying for my college expenses, and could continue to do that through the yearly income my father had been giving to each of his three daughters from one of his farms.

I was tempted to go to Tucson because I had enjoyed living there, and I would have enjoyed performing and researching in an area I knew. Also, getting a doctorate would have enabled me to acquire a teaching position at a four-year college and a prominent church position. I discussed these two possibilities with Will, who neither encouraged nor discouraged me.

I looked at the negative points of a separation: my parents would not understand my desire to continue my education instead of looking after my home, Dora would be left with more social responsibility for her father, the program would take me at least two years, it would be costly, and it would require a huge change in life for both Will and me.

On the positive side of foregoing an advanced degree: I liked my current church position. The parishioners were friendly and appreciative of my skills. The Schlicker pipe organ was a pleasure to play. But most of all, I loved our home in Los Gatos and was ready for time to relax and enjoy it, the swimming pool, and the garden.

It was fortunate for Will that I had decided to end my student days. Will was laid off from the pacemaker company after only six weeks of employment. To compensate for his lower beginning salary there, he had been given generous stock options; the company now revoked this agreement, and Will lost his health insurance as well. He sought a settlement by hiring a lawyer. Meanwhile, we were in the dangerous position of being without adequate healthcare.

I immediately sought training as a bank teller (one of my father's former occupations). Within a few months, I had secured a position close to the Lutheran church so that I could retain my job there as well. My income from both paid daily expenses and the cost of health-care insurance. Together with savings, we were able to make ends meet. Within a short time, Will had received a handsome settlement and had acquired a position to write software manuals for Honeywell Corporation. I was not expecting gratitude from him for what I had done. As the wife of an Englishman, it was my duty to keep a "stiff upper lip," to "carry on," to

"make the best of the situation."

Will's new job would not begin until September, so we had the month of August to travel to England to cheer up Clyde, who had been depressed since Laura's death. I resigned from the bank and obtained leave from the church to vacation in England. Flying into Heathrow, we rented a car, drove to Peterborough, and picked up Clyde for an eight-day tour of parts of England, including Boston, Norwich, and Bury St. Edmunds, and then across to Wales. Clyde and I became great companions. In his memoir, he wrote:

> *Beth so loved our country roads and villages. She sat with a map on her knee, and sometimes we got lost, but we eventually arrived at a town. Beth would find out the nearest cathedral or parish church, and if possible get a view of the organ. . . . Back in Peterborough, they gave me a birthday dinner at their hotel, which I shall remember always.*

Clyde had just turned eighty-six. By the end of the following May, he had died of prostate and bone cancer. In the last paragraph of his memoir, he wrote:

> *This house is much too big for me, but I shall carry on with it as long as I can. I have over one thousand color slides. I can turn any slide up at a moment's notice. I have a good library of cassettes, many of which are organ recitals by Beth. So I have plenty of things to keep me interested.*

What a sweet man he had been! After Laura died, he had tried to erase some of the bitterness she had left behind. In her will, she had left me a hand-painted fruit bowl, Dora quite a few memorable pieces of china and silver, but nothing for Will. Clyde had put Will back as the main recipient of his will, leaving him approximately fifty thousand pounds. Because Will knew how much I had grown to love his father, he bought me a beautiful antique diamond ring in remembrance of him.

In June, 1987 we returned to England for Clyde's funeral. Will was irate when a parishioner said to him following the ceremony, "You didn't really know your parents well, did you?" I silently agreed with the man. Getting to really know someone is a two-way street. Secrecy and lack of communication do not create good relationships. The one exception for Will had been our daughter, whom he had been able to partly mold into the perfect person.

We had paid Dora's expenses to come with us for Clyde's funeral and a trip following. As an adult, she had never seen much of England. We took her to areas around Peterborough and Cambridge, then to Oxford and Stratford-on-Avon, where we attended a performance of *Julius Caesar*, one she was bound to teach in her high school English classes. She was bubbling with enthusiasm, Will was having a glorious time, and I was a "third wheel." When we were sightseeing, Will and Dora (having longer legs) kept pace with each other as we walked, and I trailed behind, even when crossing a busy intersection. At meals they conversed mainly with each other. Eventually, I had had enough. I said, "Tomorrow I'm leaving. I'm going home early."

"Don't be ridiculous!" was Will's response. We spent a very quiet evening together. Having discussed the incident sometime that night with her dad, Dora said to me the next morning, "I'm going back to Peterborough to visit with the relatives. You and Dad go on to London." Will and I went to London, where we enjoyed a ballet, an opera, and a visit to Queue Gardens. Dora joined us for a final night out to dinner and a performance of *Les Miserables*.

In the spring of 1988, Kurt from Wiesbaden suddenly appeared on our doorstep. He and Will, now ten years older, were still good-looking. Kurt had remained a handsome, well-built, blond-haired bachelor. Will was distinguished-looking at age fifty-six. They obviously enjoyed each other's company while ignoring my presence. Will included me toward the end of the visit by asking me to play a few Chopin waltzes on the piano. When Kurt commented that he had never liked any classical music, I felt like playing a difficult Bach fugue for his further enjoyment!

When Kurt left, I asked Will, who had liked *only* classical music, how he could have enjoyed all of the folk music festivals when he was in Wiesbaden. A shrug of his shoulders was the only explanation I got for Will's 1978 mystery trip to Wiesbaden.

During the summer of 1988, problems arose at the Lutheran church, where I had been employed for eight years. A debate among the church leadership developed regarding the upholstering of the hard wooden pews. The older members of the congregation wanted the comfort of soft seats and backs. Those who appreciated music over comfort were worried about the effect of the upholstery on the acoustics.

I was asked to research the acoustical effect on the sound of the organ and the choral music. Will added his knowledge of physics to the report for the committee, which was composed of the clergy, selected members of the board of elders, and the financial officers of the church. Several members of the group were also singers in the adult choir. The final meeting was held in an upstairs room. Will was invited to accompany me. After questions, answers, and debate, the committee voted to approve the upholstery.

Will hurled angry insults about lack of understanding and disregard for music, then stomped out of the room and stumbled noisily down the stairs. Did he expect me to follow him? I sat shaken, the only female in the room, while the remaining males stared at me in amazement.

Throughout the summer, I was encouraged by members of various music groups, parishioners, and the pastor to remain in my position, but too much animosity had been created within the church. I left for a similar position in another Lutheran church. Even though Will felt, again, that he needed to sing in the choir and ring in the bell choir, I watched carefully so that he had no opportunity to control my position, either openly or behind the scenes.

In September, 1992 our first grandchild, Sara, was born. Dora chose Will's middle name, Parker, a family surname, as Sara's middle name, honoring Will and the English relations.

I took two weeks off from church to care for Dora and the baby when they came home from the hospital in Manteca. My mother had helped me to recuperate from childbirth, and I wanted to carry on the tradition. I enabled Dora to get bed rest and enjoy her newborn while I attended to their house and the preparation of the meals.

Vince was working part-time and going to college again. (He had partied too much at the time that Dora had gotten her degree. She had been teaching for six years, bringing in the major portion of their income.) Unfortunately, Vince had not overcome his drinking problem. While I was cleaning one day, I found a dozen empty rum bottles behind the sofa in the living room. Although I just left them there and said nothing about it, he realized that I had seen them. The next morning Dora told me that Vince and she felt that she could handle Sara better on her own and asked me to leave.

When I came home early, I poured out my hurt and grief to Will, but he had no empathy for me. In the months following, I did not try to make amends for something I had not done, and Dora did not contact me at all. I remained sick at heart. That incident came immediately to mind many years later when I read a poem of consolation that Will had written to Mary in March, 1960, expressing the feelings of a tender lover and a humble friend:

"Prayer"
Am I Thine—I know not,
Perhaps once I was—

Make of her my guiding light,
My shining star,
My guardian angel.

Make of me, a humble and honest friend,
A tender lover,
A strong and fearless challenge
To the troubles of a troubled world.

With her by my side
And with Thee for our God,
We can each to the other
Give the love
Which is the power for living.

"Tender love" or just "humble and honest" friendship would have helped me during this time of separation from our daughter. It was Dora who eventually reached out to me to begin to repair our broken relationship.

In September, 1993, a year and a week after Sara's birth, my father died unexpectedly of a massive cerebral hemorrhage. By the time I arrived in Nebraska, he was still on a respirator even though he had been pronounced brain-dead. Mother did not want to take the final move of having the respirator detached until her three daughters were with her.

I stayed with Mother for a month. Together we chose Dad's casket and planned the funeral and the reception following. Mother knew that because Dad had been such a well-known and respected businessman, many people would come to pay tribute to him.

Following the funeral, burial, and reception for guests, I stayed in Nebraska with Mother to help her with thank-you notes, business papers, clearing out files, etc. When I returned to California, I continued to call Mother several times a week to help her with her grief. I found that encouraging her to talk about memories of her years with Dad and memories of her own childhood and adult life helped her to temporarily feel better. As she relayed the past to me, I jotted down notes, which I later used to write a family memoir.

My sister, Amy, who lived in Lincoln, convinced Mother to sell her property and move to a rental home near Amy. Mother made the move in December, but by

June, she was deeply depressed. Loss of husband, home, church, and old friends was too much for her. I traveled to Nebraska again for a month's stay in Lincoln. By the end of the month, she had decided to move back to the area where she had lived for sixty-one years with her husband. There she would be among friends, living in a retirement complex. During the two separate months of my absence from our California home, Will had had plenty of opportunities to be a "bachelor" again. Apparently, he had been contented, perhaps happy, without me.

At Christmastime, my sister Nancy came for a visit. She was still suffering from an unhappy divorce and was looking for a little joy and companionship. While she was with us, a bachelor friend of Will's appeared one evening for a visit. I had never met George, and Will had never mentioned him. Like Kurt, George was handsome and about ten years younger than Will. We decided to go to a dinner-dance restaurant for the evening. At a table for four, George sat with Nancy to one side and Will to the other; I sat opposite George. The mealtime conversation was almost exclusively between Will and George. Occasionally, Nancy reached out to George, touching his arm at one point, but received no response. No one danced during the evening.

When we got back home, Will invited George in, Nancy excused herself for the night, and Will then apologized to George for Nancy's behavior. What apology was needed? I excused myself and left Will and George to themselves.

I went to bed thinking about our marital relationship. I thought about the evening we had just experienced and about the visit that Nancy and I had had about our marriages. Her former husband had been *openly* unfaithful to her, but Will was secretive and sometimes deceitful. I relayed to Nancy that Will had often bragged about how he and a group of coworkers had deceived their employer during their skiing days in Colorado. At the end of the workday, one had remained behind and worked overtime for time-and-a-half pay. Being unsupervised, he had filled out the time chart for overtime for each of the group. They had daily alternated in perpetuating this scheme.

Nancy agreed with me that Will had psychological, perhaps physical, reasons for his behavior. These may have led to his refusal to see a marriage counselor. I wondered if Will even understood his own feelings. Nancy and I concluded that only a professional could understand Will's nature.

Chapter 10

STILL FRIENDS

❧

From 1994 through 1997, our marriage continued on a friendship basis. Our common shared interests were church, music, family, and travel. During these years, we took delightful trips to Canada, including Montreal, Quebec, Banff, Lake Louise, Emerald Lake, Vancouver, and Victoria. One of my favorite spots was the Butchardt Gardens on Victoria Island.

Within the gardens, I was enthralled with a gorgeous tiered area that occupied a former quarry. It had been landscaped into different levels with a path leading from the top level down to the bottom; thus, one could view the flowers and shrubbery from several aspects. If any place could reignite a romantic flame for me, that was it. However, I sat alone on various benches set along the path while Will took photos.

Will's favorite area was the large rose garden. Among the hundreds of varieties of roses were many individual plants named after famous people from England: members of the royalty, prime ministers, actors and actresses, musicians, etc. I was surprised at Will's interest in roses. For years, I had expressed my love of roses and had often wanted a bouquet of roses or even a single rose for my birthday. Will had always claimed to be allergic to them.

When we were on our eight-day trip with his father, Clyde and I often sought out a beautiful English garden within a town. We strolled together, arms linked, to enjoy the roses and flowers along the paths. Roses had become a bond between us.

After Will's death, I pieced together the knowledge that roses had had a double meaning for Will — the flower and a lost love. Several years following his emigration to Canada, in 1958, Will had returned to England for a summer vacation and had fallen in love with Gisela.

Laura had encouraged the romance, thinking that Will, then twenty-five, would want to settle down in England. But Will wanted Gisela to leave her family and join him in Toronto, a move she refused to make. Her rejection of him had put her on a pedestal. Unlike the American girls he was soon to pursue in the "skiing world," she remained pure.

His poem "English Roses" had not been addressed to her, but the date coincides with that of a picture of Laura and Clyde standing next to Will and Gisela, with their arms around each other. A brief notation underneath the photo in the album said, "Vacation at Skegness"—one of Clyde and Laura's favorite seaside holiday spots.

"English Roses"

I gave my love on Monday
A rose of scarlet hue:
Elusive as the pimpernel
My wayward rosebud grew.

I gave my love on Tuesday
A perfect crimson rose:
To hint how much I loved her
- A fact which well she knows.

And then again on Wednesday,
A blood-red rose I gave—
Despair became my portion:

The love for which I crave.

I gave to her on Thursday
A rose of purest white—
A token of surrender;
My prayer throughout the night

That when I came on Friday
A carmine rose to give;
My prayer would have been answered
- Our nourished love would live.

And Saturday came smiling,
The rose a brilliant red:
My happy heart was laughing
- Our love by no means dead.

On Sunday I stepped gaily,
A golden rose my gift:
Its purpose in the giving
To end and heal our rift.

In 1998, at the age of sixty-six, Will began to experience symptoms of prostate enlargement, including frequent urination and high PSA levels. Following examination and tests by a doctor of urology, Will was diagnosed with stage-one cancer of the prostate. It was a fast-growing cancer, and by the time Will had surgery, the cancer had spread to surrounding tissue. Radiation treatment followed. At a later visit with the urologist, the doctor asked Will if he would like an implant to enable an erection of the penis. Will reported to me that his response to the doctor had been, "My wife and I have been long past that for many years." I was only sixty-three, but his insensitive words made me feel twenty years older, almost lifeless. I recalled that feeling again when I found his cheerful sonnet "Merry Goes the Earth," dedicated to a mysterious Marylou in the spring before his surgery. She was perhaps a coworker of his.

"Merry Goes the Earth"
To Marylou

Merry goes the Earth around her orbit;
Attracted by the Sun, she spins in bliss;
Revolving smartly like a child's toy top.

Years pass swiftly, and the dance continues.
Light bathes her body as she dances free
Of any constraint but whispering clouds—
Unheeding other suns or other earths.

Observe our blue planet spinning away,
Circled by her "lifeless" friend, the moon:
Totally inert?—Yet maybe, not so!—
Deep in her dust organisms may still live,
Reluctant to grow or to show themselves.

Rejoice in your spin, enjoying your dance
With your lunar friend until music's end!

One medical problem that definitely plagued Will following his surgery was urinary incontinence. When minor surgeries for this were unsuccessful, Will resorted to the use of the Cunningham Clamp, which can be manually attached at the base of the penis to prevent leakage of urine. Since leakage does not occur when the body is in a prone position, the device can be unclamped at bedtime.

Will endured some discomfort when using the device, but he made the most he could out of sympathy from other males. Our son-in-law, Vince, thought it hilarious when Will, while playing poker with Vince and his buddies, suddenly withdrew an unused Cunningham Clamp from the pocket of his sports coat, showed it around the table, and asked them to guess what it was. When Will explained it, the look on their faces was priceless. They did not have the reaction of sympathy that Will had expected. Perhaps he should have also handed them a copy of his acrostic poem, explaining the device, along with his brave way of coping with it:

"The Cunningham Clamp"

C *Can there be anything more beautiful—*
U *Unless, with care, you look beneath the skin—*
N *Noticing pregnant pods and fruit within—*
N *Nothing less than pain's end: and so begin*
I *In peace and love and spirit dutiful*
N *Not to think bad thoughts, but each sad-glad day,*
G *Gaining more acceptance, in ev'ry way*
H *Holding on to truth for truth's sake:*
A *And still the piper's costly fee to pay—*
M *Making the best of unspeakable times.*

C   *Come! Snap out of morbid soliloquies!—*
L   *Leave behind "sad sack" groans for better climes,*
A   *And smiles and laughs your downcast visage take,*
M   *Making yourself and others happy. 'Tis*
P   *Pantagruel's achievement—fresh water lake!**

* Rabelais' "Gargantua et Pantagruel"

In May 2000, Will needed his third open-heart surgery. Since his second valve replacement in 1985, his aortic heart valve had again re-calcified. Surgeons were no longer using homografts from cadavers; consequently, Will's valve was replaced with a St. Jude titanium valve, which required him to be on a blood thinner for the rest of his life. Once again I had to be nursemaid and mother as he awaited his surgery and then recuperated from it. It was more difficult for me this time at age sixty-five. I was finishing my career as a musician in a church where I had worked for ten years while preparing for a move to Manteca, to be near Dora and her family. I had planned for the moving van and Will's operation to be at least two weeks apart. However, the hospital rescheduled his surgery for moving day, and I found myself trying to be at two different locations on the same day.

After Will was released from the hospital, I drove him to our new home in Manteca, where the moving boxes were waiting in the garage while our furniture was temporarily stored in a warehouse. Will was unable to help me as I unpacked each box and gradually turned the house into a home.

Our main reason for selling our delightful home in Los Gatos and moving to the less cultural, rural town of Manteca was to help Dora and Vince with their hectic teaching and parental schedules. Vince had overcome alcoholism, had finished college, and was now employed as a math teacher in Danville, fifty miles from Manteca; Dora was employed as an English teacher in Tracy, twenty miles from home; and their three children were attending different schools in or near Manteca—one in preschool, one in lower elementary, and one in upper elementary. Will and I took on the roles of maid, babysitter, and chauffeur. Once Will had recovered from his surgery, he resumed his job as a technical writer from his home computer; consequently, most of the care of the grandchildren became my responsibility.

My daily schedule was hectic: I had to be dressed for the day and have breakfast ready for the older children by 6:00 AM, when Dora dropped them off on her way to school. School didn't begin for them until 9:00. I monitored homework and piano lessons after breakfast while preparing bag lunches for the day. Once a week, each of them received a piano lesson from me. If time permitted, Will and I played cards with them, alternating between Knock-out Whist, which Will's father had taught him, Old Maid, and Seven-up, which my mother had taught me. At the end of the day, I picked them up from school, helped them with their homework at our house, and babysat them until Dora picked them up at the end of the afternoon.

Sometimes during the week, Will or I had to take one or more of the children for pediatric or dental appointments. I often was called upon to take Dora's place as parent for a school performance. Accidents at school or sick days called for special attention.

My weekly schedule provided little free time for me. I had not given up professional music and had accepted the position of organist and choir director in a church in Turlock, about thirty miles away. While the kids were in school, I drove to Turlock to practice the organ or to prepare choral music. One evening per week, Will and

I attended choir rehearsal at the church. Saturday was both organ practice and housekeeping day for me, and Sunday was church for both of us.

In my music position, I was asked to give an annual organ concert at the church. This encouraged me to keep up my technique and skills, and I usually followed the concert in Turlock by giving a similar concert at the Episcopal Cathedral in Reno, Nevada—an enjoyable weekend outing for Will and me. In addition to these public concerts, I helped the grandchildren to prepare a family recital at Thanksgiving or Christmastime. I combined these occasions with a family dinner while Will prepared a cute program on the computer. All in all, it was a time of busy activity and contentment for us.

Fear of death for Robbie, the youngest, replaced contentment when a brain tumor attached to his pituitary gland was diagnosed by the pediatrician. By the time of his first surgery in San Diego, the tumor had grown to the size of an orange. Since the pituitary is located at the back of the skull, the surgeons had to split his skull from ear to ear, lift up the brain, and then remove the tumor. A year later, at age six, the surgery was repeated because the tumor had regrown. When it regrew a third time, Vince took Robbie to Boston for three months of radiation. The hospital there had a machine that could pinpoint the radiation from the height of two stories, enabling more accuracy and less damage to the brain. Although the tumor did not regrow, Robbie lost his pituitary gland, which is the major control of other glands and organs within the body. As a result, Robbie was left with a lifetime of daily replacement medication and expensive follow-up examinations.

All of this took a tremendous toll on the other members of the family. Dora and Vince became very protective parents, and Will and I sometimes felt as though we were "walking on eggshells." We tried from time to time to lighten the atmosphere for the girls by taking them on excursions away from home.

When Sara was seven and Sue three, we took them on outings close to Manteca, sometimes to play miniature golf in Modesto, sometimes to a nearby small zoo. When they were a year older, we ventured to San Francisco to see Fisherman's Wharf or to go for a boat ride on the bay. On one occasion we were on BART (Bay Area Rapid Transit), sitting close to the rear door of the car. When the train halted at one of the stops along the way, four-year-old Sue sprang up from her seat and was nearly out the door before I could grab hold of her dress—a grandmother's nightmare.

On another excursion, when Robbie was well enough to accompany us, I drove us to San Francisco for a day at the Exploratorium Museum for Children. Will's job had been to plot the location of the museum on a map from his computer and to navigate once we were in San Francisco. That day he was in one of his "wot not" moods. He couldn't find the location, and yet he wouldn't take suggestions from either Sara or me. We wandered around for several hours, with Sara and Sue calling out street names from the back seat. At one point, we had to stop at a convenience store so that Robbie could urinate. The store had no restroom! I had to shelter Robbie from view as he relieved himself against the wheel of the car. We finally gave up on Will's map, which was incorrect. (Will's map showed the Exploratorium located on a street that didn't exist.) Stopping at a gas station, we got the correct location of the museum, arriving in time for a visit of a few hours before we had to head home. The children had enjoyed the whole experience as a lark! Will's humorous poem, written in 1960 about famous Englishmen "wot nots" still reminds me of Will and his map:

"James Watt and Christopher Wren"

James Watt
>*Knew not what.*
>>*He wot not.*

Christopher Wren
>*Thought that Big Ben*
>>*Should be built again.*

Thomas Carlyle
>*Thought it the style*
>>*To philosophize awhile.*

The Elder Pitt
>*A man without wit*
>>*In Parliament did sit.*

Since Will's death, our grandchildren have often remembered him humorously, enjoying his "wot not" characteristic and his high intelligence expressed in "quirky" ways.

All of the vigilance and care we gave to the grand-children could have resulted in Dora's gratitude toward both Will and me. However, although Dora badly needed my help, she would have preferred being home with her children, and I had assumed the daily role of mother. I could understand her feelings, with memories of my relationship with Laura when she took the role of mother. For me, though, this was a time when I was the most giving, and the children benefitted from it. Through my academic tutoring and piano lessons, the children received advantages they could not have otherwise had. When Sara, the oldest, won the top academic award at her graduation from the eighth grade, the principal singled out Will and me as examples of generational help.

Will had played a less active role in the care of the grandchildren, but Dora showed her gratitude by preparing a dinner at her home for Father's Day and another for Will's birthday. At these times, she "went to town for him," as Clyde would have said. She always made his favorite entrée, roast beef and Yorkshire pudding, and his favorite dessert, bread pudding. Sometimes she took him out for "afternoon tea" at a local shop carrying English specialties. Toward the end of our time in Manteca, Robbie and I were invited to enjoy the tea occasion with Dora and Will. At the end of the tea, consisting of a pot of tea for each of us, tiny sandwiches, and trays of sweets, we were all stuffed. Will took the opportunity to recite one of his poems:

"On Overeating—"

The signal that the meal has ended—
The candles blown—the guests unbended,
Standing up and groaning so:
You've eaten far too much you know!
Your figure slim . . . before the feast,
But stay content—you're full at least;
Forget the line so smooth and pretty—
You can't eat more . . . and more's the pity.

Chapter 11

THE OCTOGENARIAN

When school was over for the summer months, Dora and Vince were again in full-time charge of the children. Will and I were alone once more and took the opportunity for a summer holiday, each year going somewhere far from Manteca, such as Germany, Austria, or Switzerland. Now older, we both felt more comfortable on group trips where the planning was in the hands of the tour guide.

On our first evening in Frankfurt, we met Carl, a single retired Latin teacher from upper New York State and his cousin, Father John, a priest from Toronto. They invited Will, but not me, to spend the evening with them. I politely objected, and for the remainder of the trip, we often became a group of three men and me. I was capable of discussing their like interests of religion, art, music, literature, nature, geography, and history. There were a few bawdy jokes and stories with me in their presence, but I managed to keep our small group politely social.

We stayed friends for years, visiting each other in our individual homes in Manteca, Toronto, and the Finger Lakes area of northern New York State. Before Fr. John died a year later, we joined in a grand tour of Italy. This time, Cora, Carl's female, single cousin joined us, having just retired as a teacher. We traveled throughout Italy on a bus. Since there was a daily rotation of seats, we asked the tour guide to arrange the chart so that each of the five of us could have equal visitation opportunities as we traveled. I noticed that Will engaged in lively conversation when he sat next to Fr. John, Carl, or Cora. When Will was next to me, he insisted on the window seat, turned away from me, and took pictures throughout the ride. When we stopped to tour a site on foot, Fr. John and Cora, the slowest walkers, stayed together while Will, Carl, and I walked ahead. It was not long before Will took off on his own with his camera.

Our trip ended in Venice. We five spent most of the last day visiting St. Mark's Cathedral. During an afternoon snack and a rest in the cathedral square, I asked

Will to take me for a ride in one of the gondolas parked nearby. Being a romantic, I had visualized that experience for years. Will ignored me. I waited patiently for a break in the conversation and then repeated my request. Finally, after about five entreaties, Fr. John said, "Will, for heaven's sake, take your wife for a gondola ride!"

Since Will couldn't ignore *him*, we headed for a gondola. The ride was a romantic disaster. Will immediately got out his camera and took photos throughout the ride, never putting an arm around me. When we returned to the others, who looked questioningly at us, Will simply remarked, "The water was green and polluted." This ride was an unimportant event in relation to all that a couple of fifty-two years had experienced, but it shows yet another change in attitude. I had become not just a piece of furniture in the privacy of our home but a wooden bench in public as well, an object to be used only when needed. I am reminded of Will's poem to Carol, written in May 1959:

"What Do I Offer You?"

What do I offer you?
Wealth?   No.
Fame?   No, indeed!

I offer you my need of you.
I offer you a chance
To enjoy enduring love and devotion,
A chance to share
My joy and emotion.

For me, there had not been wealth, fame, enduring love and devotion, or joy and emotion. The line best fitting our relationship is, "I offer you_my_ need of you." At times Will had been very needy because of his health and his inability to remain centered, but whenever his needs had been met, love and devotion, or sharing his emotions, had not followed.

After Fr. John died, Will and Carl remained friends until Will's death. They corresponded regularly through the Internet. Both enjoyed serious religious and secular topics and, contrastingly, humorous, off-color articles. Will enjoyed sending Carl poems he had written, such as his "take-off" on "The Owl and the Pussycat."

"A Harlot and a Bishop"

A harlot and a bishop went out one day,

132

In a coach with a team of four,
They stopped in a field of fresh-mown hay—
And the bishop he opened the door.
She chased him around, and was gaining ground—
What a strange, strange sight to see:
And there in a wood, the harlot she stood—
And the bishop had climbed up a tree,
A tree—a tree!
And the bishop had climbed up a tree.

A serious time ensued for Will and me when my mother died in March 2013 in a nursing home in Nebraska. This became a time when Will and I needed each other. Mother was one hundred, the last of her generation in the family. I experienced grief not only for her but for all who had gone before her.

For the funeral, I flew to Nebraska with Dora. While we were there, the administrator of Mother's estate avoided discussing the will or financial matters at the time that family members were all in Nebraska. However, a month later, I was informed of the change that had been made to Mother's will when she was already well into Alzheimer's. My parents had jointly planned for each daughter to receive one of their three farms, leaving the choice of the farm up to each of us. Although the estate had been rich in liquid assets as well as property when Mother entered the nursing home, there was no longer enough cash to settle it when she died eighteen months later. Consequently, the administrator planned to sell one of the farms for the needed cash, making it impossible for each daughter to receive one of the promised farms.

Will was as unsettled with this scenario as I was. Since California is a community property state, the farm would become his as well as mine. When he married me, he knew that I would eventually prove to be a good economic "catch." Now was the time to work together to secure our economic future; Will and I temporarily became a team again. I hired a Nebraska lawyer, who subpoenaed financial records that he then sent to me. I organized all of the material for the next six months, and Will mathematically analyzed the data and recorded it on the computer. Together we used his skills in math and analysis and mine in English and organization to produce some convincing documents and charts to be used in the lawsuit. Fortunately, we were able to settle the estate without going to trial; Will and I were now owners of a farm. Once more, we had worked successfully together.

In 2014, with two grandchildren in college and Robbie about to finish high school, Will and I were no longer needed as substitute parents. It was time to move from our big house in Manteca to a humbler home. After researching different geographical areas within the U.S., we chose Santa Fe, New Mexico, because of its beauty and culture. Not long after our move, we found a spiritually alive and musically satisfying church to join.

During 2015 we entertained family visitors to Santa Fe. In June Dora came with Sue and Robbie for a five-day visit. All went well during the first three days. We took them sightseeing in Santa Fe, including the cathedral, the plaza, and Museum Hill. Then we introduced them to surrounding areas. The second day we visited the Bandolier National Monument, where the ancient cliff dwellings are located. While Will sat on a bench, Dora, Sue, Robbie, and I climbed up wooden ladders to explore the inside of the dwellings. Like Dora had done in England, she left me behind while she went ahead with her children. At one point, a tourist said to me, "Let me help you." He remained at the base of the ladder until I had safely returned. Dora, embarrassed that a stranger had helped me, became more attentive to me as we continued. On the third day, after a beautiful drive through the Jemez Mountains and Los Alamos, we stopped for hamburgers in a restaurant on our way home. Dora kept searching for information about why we had decided to move. Among the reasons for our move, I finally admitted that Will and I had not felt needed anymore in Manteca. Will sat silent; everybody became silent.

We all went to bed that evening with more plans for sightseeing the next day. Early the next morning, Will excitedly awakened me, announcing, "They're leaving!" I put on my housecoat and walked into the living room to find everyone dressed, ready to go, bags packed. We sat down for a moment, and Dora explained that they were leaving because I had been unbelievably unkind to them. Turning to Will, she added, "Nobody ever likes Mom." Will's only response was to sob. After they had left, Will's sorrow turned to anger. When the family later called from the road, he angrily threatened them, "You'll be sorry for this!"

In the five months that followed, there was no communication between Dora and us. Will and I said little about the matter. However, the estrangement simmered in my mind, like a cup of coffee brewing on the stove. I thought about my lost time with Dora when she was a baby and I was too ill to take care of her. After Laura and Clyde had returned to England, I had remained in teaching and had become too busy to give Dora as much attention as she needed while Will had developed a childhood bond with her—one that remained in Dora's memory as lovely bedtime singing and verses from Santa and the tooth fairy. For Will, she had been the center of attention in our home (her portrait was there to prove it), and Will had encouraged her love by addressing her as "Darling" while she heard me addressed as "Beth." I had been jealous of Will's love for Dora. Dora, too, had many reasons for being envious of me. I had been a difficult role model for her to follow: I had pursued further education; she wanted to but couldn't. I had had a successful career in music; she loved music but did not have enough time for it. Will and I had achieved economic success; she and Vince were always struggling financially. I had taken care of her young children; she had wanted to be home with them. Finally, she thought that I had encouraged her beloved father to move away from her and her family.

Actually, our decision to move to Santa Fe had been a joint one, but until now, Will had not been part of the "pot that boiled over." However, Will had always had difficulty looking at a situation from the point of view of another, and Dora was somewhat like that too. It was up to me to take the first step to repair the rift. For Dora's birthday, in November, I suggested to Will that we send Dora two dozen yellow roses as a peace offering. He was overjoyed! When the bouquet arrived, Dora gladly accepted our gift of love.

Our second family visitors were my sister Amy and her husband Mike. Will and I again became sight-seeing tour guides. I had also prepared a private organ concert for them at the church because they had never heard me perform. Since it was not a public concert, Will did not bother to listen to it but wandered about the church environs taking pictures and visiting with anyone in the area.

One evening the four of us sat down after supper for a game of bridge—a big mistake! Since his college days, Will had been an aggressive bridge player. In Toronto he had played duplicate bridge and had entered, and won, tournaments and awards. After we were married, he continued playing against the computer, read daily columns in the newspaper, and wrote poems or entered notes about bridge in one of his many notebooks on various topics.

I had been interested only in social bridge, played mainly for fun. Throughout the years, we had played bridge at times with my parents and sometimes with a church or social group. Years earlier on a visit to Nebraska, we had played with Amy and Mike, and because of Will's aggressive style and skill, we had "trounced" them. Will was looking forward to a similar event this time.

However, Amy and Mike had become duplicate bridge players. I had not played for years and could barely remember much about bidding. As the game progressed, Will became increasingly angry with me, insulting me and scowling at me. Letting the devil have his way, I suddenly bid *eight* No Trump, an impossible bid. Will threw down his cards and almost struck me; Amy and Mike laughed.

This scenario describes a petty incident, but it illustrates another aspect of our relationship. Will cared more about how he appeared as a bridge player than he did about our marriage. Among his autobiographical sketches that he had written before his death, he had included one titled "Will Takes Up Contract Bridge"

*Soon after I arrived in Toronto, I joined
a bridge club that met twice a week at*

the west end of Bloor Street. To get there from Orchard View Boulevard I took the subway train down to the Bloor Street streetcar and took it to the Bloor Street west terminus. This took an hour each way. (Wouldn't you know it? —Now there is a Bloor Street subway line!)

Being a newcomer I paired with an individual that, after each hand, analyzed every play to the nth degree. I played with this person for about three months and grinned and bore it. Then the organizers of the club decided to have an individual tournament. My erstwhile partner came in second from bottom, but I came in third from top. (I think there were about twelve tables, so that made 48 players.) Guess what! —One of the top five players adopted me as his regular partner. After that, we "placed" at every meet, sometimes first but never lower than third.

The next thing that happened was that eight of us decided to play teams of four. I remember one hand where my partner bid to six of his major suit (hotly contested by the opposition all the way). I had passed every round until the last, when I bid seven. My reason was that if he could bid six without my Ace of Trumps, I could bid seven with it. A gamble, yes, but even more of a gamble when we were doubled and my partner redoubled! My partner made the contract, doubled, redoubled and vulnerable! The score: 120 per trick, 100 for insult, 1500 for grand slam bonus and 700 for a two-game rubber = 840 +100+1500+700=3140, which, incidentally, is the maximum that can be made on a hand in a major suit. (7 No Trump would have added 40 for 3180 points, but 3140 ain't bad.)

So what is the golden rule for playing bridge? Have a solid understanding of

*the game, choose a good partner, and
trust one another.*

I was neither a good choice of partner for him in bridge nor in any other intellectual pursuit, with the exception of Scrabble. On the computer, Will had left a message in bold, extremely large print, no doubt for me:

"Marriage is like a deck of cards. In the beginning all you need is two hearts and a diamond. By the end you wish you had a club and spade."

When I first read this, I stewed about it for a while. Then I realized that losing so badly to Amy and Mike had wounded Will's intellectual pride. Throughout most of his lifetime, he had striven to improve his skills in bridge, and I had made him look like a fool. It is a shame that Will died before he could understand my point of view about the game, which I expressed in a poem, turning his harsh words into a lesson about married life:

"The Hand Dealt"

*Marriage begins like
    A deck of cards.
In the beginning you need
    Two hearts and a diamond.*

By the end of the game
  You may wish you'd had
  A club and a spade.

The entire game
  Depends not on
  The hand first dealt,
But on how each partner
  Has played.

During Christmas of 2015, my niece Maggie and Sylvia, her nine-year-old daughter, flew from Nebraska to visit us. Maggie was especially interested in spending time in the cathedral and the square in downtown Santa Fe, and in hearing me play a short organ recital for her at our nearby church. Maggie, a professional violinist, had brought her fine violin with her. We enjoyed playing violin and piano together at our home. Will, always addicted to his computer, never came into the living room to listen to us. He had once been a violinist but had not played for years and was not interested in watching Maggie perform. However, he was interested in displaying his skills in poetry and a series of creative

143

"happy face" pictures he had made on the computer. Nine-year-old Sylvia found these amusing.

Maggie had appreciated the high-desert terrain of Santa Fe, ringed by mountains, and the wild plants that grew here. Will wrote a poem, which he dedicated to her. It describes Will's favorite cactus on our rural lot:

"Cholla"
(a sonnet for Maggie)

Cholla is a cactus of great beauty
Here in New Mexico's desert landscape—
Growing sometimes to fifteen feet in height;
Yet a plant that whispers, "Do not touch me!"
Its spines can be a painful reminder—
"Touch me not!" it says again and again—
Sharp merciless spines imbed in your skin—
Not a sweet memory or loving touch!
Ecoutez-moi—I can't stress it too much!

Still its great beauty makes up for its pain—
Rosy blooms appear mid and late July
On its spiny stretched-out limbs and branches,
Whisp'ring, "Enjoy me—I'll soon disappear!"
Nascent harbingers of its yellow fruit.

After Maggie and Sylvia returned to Nebraska, Maggie called us weekly. If Will answered the phone, he always had five or six of his poems to read to her, some of them passionate poems from his Colorado skiing days. He did not reveal to her the name of the person to whom he had dedicated the poem, nor the year he had written it. Maggie naturally assumed that his passion had been for me, not others, like Joan:

"Hopeless Passion"
To X

I fell in love with you—
So quickly—could it be true?
And yet to me it seems
That you're too often in my dreams.

I'm loath to understand;
Yet on the other hand
There's not a girl I've ever met,
Who on her own I'd rather get.

We talked for just an hour,
And I was in your power:
I loved you then as no one else could—
I loved you then as I never should.

After Will had read this poem to Maggie, she said to him, "You must have really loved Aunt Beth," to which he answered, "Oh, I wrote that for a friend of mine who needed some inspiration." Deceit, still at age eighty-three! Later, after Will's death, Maggie admitted to me that she had found the relationship between Will and me a strained one. Our house had been a very quiet one. Not surprising! A computer and a piece of furniture have little to say to each other.

Chapter 12

FINAL DAYS

᠁᠁᠁

*I*n May, 2016 I made one last attempt to divert Will's attention from the computer back to me. I needed to visit my farm in Nebraska, and I suggested to him that we include the farm on an extensive car trip throughout the Midwest, driving to areas we had been many years prior or to some we had never seen. It was a long trip through Eastern Colorado, Kansas, Missouri, Wisconsin, Michigan, Iowa, and Nebraska. From St. Louis, we followed the Mississippi River north to the Great Lakes area. While in St. Louis, we stayed at an elegant five-star hotel overlooking the Mississippi River. Our room on the tenth floor had a breathtaking view of the river barges and bridges at night. Our cat, Lovey, enjoyed looking out the picture window at the activity below.

I had suggested taking seventeen-year-old Lovey along for companionship, hopefully to inspire some tender moments for Will. Lovey was like a tonic. While I drove, Lovey, sitting on Will's lap, encouraged him to love and to be loved. Will was quiet throughout the trip, but it had had a positive effect on our relationship. Sometime after our return to Santa Fe, he had written a message for me on his computer, again in large print: "I thank God for my wonderful, accomplished, fun to be with, loving wife of 56 years, many of them difficult, but with her many capabilities we have overcome the vicissitudes, and I look forward to a healthier and happier life for us both in 2017 and beyond."

Unfortunately, he never gave the message to me, and I did not find it until after his death.

Not long after we were back from our trip, Will reverted to his dual personality, the public Will and the private, self-absorbed Will. In public he was an extrovert, seeking attention from even strangers when he recited one of his poems. At church he sought the attention of attractive women for conversation or praise for his reading of the Old Testament or the Epistle lesson of the day. At home he communicated via the Internet. The house was deathly silent.

Will's false public display of regard for me was revealed one Sunday at the coffee hour following church. I was visiting with a friend of mine when Will interrupted our conversation by putting an arm around my shoulders and kissing me on the cheek. My friend exclaimed, "What a sweet, loving husband you have!" I had had decades of this kind of false display, and I spouted out the truth, saying, "He only does that in public!"

Once I had called him out on his false display of love for me, it was not long before he ceased to be even polite toward me. Already frail in health, he frequently needed me to drive him during the night to the emergency ward, where I sat with him until he got the diagnosis and subsequent care he needed. There was never a thank-you to me during or after these long vigils. I was just a part of the metal chair at his bedside. Sometimes he was admitted for an overnight stay in the hospital and I was able to go home to my own bed. When I returned the next day for a visit, I found him cheerfully engaged with a nurse or a visitor, and I sat nearby as an onlooker.

A serious fall in the autumn of 2017 landed him in the hospital again. After a series of tests, the doctor determined that a blood vessel had broken in his right lung, which had filled with a pint of blood. When he had regained the function of his lung, they released him but had scheduled him for a series of further tests.

A week after his eighty-fifth birthday, in October, we received news that Will had extensive bone cancer, a metastasis of his earlier prostate cancer. We saw a doctor who specialized in radiology; the cancer, he said, was too advanced for treatment by radiation. Various oncologists were consulted, hormone treatment was tried, but the cancer continued to rapidly advance.

One night at home, Will angrily demanded that I immediately drive him to the hospital, where he was put onto an oxygen machine. Following a two-day stay, he was released, not to return home but to a terminal care home in Bernalillo, where he would be transported by an ambulance. I drove to the care home, signed papers, waited for the arrival of the ambulance, and watched as Will was hooked up to an oxygen machine and made comfortable in his room. When I bid him good night, he did not respond.

As I left and drove the seventy miles home, I felt guilty about the forthright and cruel statement I had made to him several weeks earlier: "I want you to know that you have deprived me of a lifetime of love." He looked at me with a blank, piercing stare and started to walk away. I stopped him, saying, "I want you to know *why* I feel that way." As I began to give him a few examples, he turned on his heel and left the room. While I drove, I wondered if he would now attempt to make peace or at least to express his feelings.

The next day, his requests to me were to buy him a laptop computer, have a member of the Geek Squad come to our home in Santa Fe, copy everything from his home computer onto the laptop, and set up a communication ability between the two computers. It was a tall order, but I thought that he was finally going to communicate with me, at least by email. I purchased the laptop and accessories, had the copy and the setup accomplished, and delivered everything to him within several days. He began fiddling with the laptop immediately, forgetting to thank me for the purchase, process, or effort I had taken.

I gave him a few days to adjust to it, and then I asked him if he had gotten used to his new device. He answered that it was too unlike his home computer, and he probably wouldn't use it. This was hard for me to believe of a man who had spent most of his adult life with various computers and was an expert at developing and using software. I suggested that I call a member of the Geek Squad to visit him in his room, but he said,

"Just let it go." (After he had died, I gave the laptop to our grandson, who found that Will had been communicating with the home computer. Will had deleted some files, changed some, and had emailed and sent copies to various people via the home or laptop computer.)

During the last five weeks of Will's life, a daily routine developed: Visitors from Santa Fe came in the morning. When Will was alone, he read, wrote, watched television (or used the computer). Medical visits and care from the staff were around-the-clock. I visited in the afternoon, bringing him his requests for special food or other items. While I was with him, he enjoyed playing Scrabble, a game requiring little verbal communication between us. I watched him eat his evening meal and then left to get home before dark.

Will's reading choices were probably unusual for someone close to death. I had purchased him a mystery for diverting his attention from self and also a spiritual book for comfort and meditation. He ignored these. He read his daily devotionals on Biblical passages, but he devoted most of his reading time to a thick volume of seventeenth- and eighteenth-century English poems that had been given to him by an anglophile from church. He continued to write poems of his own on his laptop. As late as three weeks before his death, he retained the mental ability to write an acrostic sonnet, called "Prostate Cancer":

P	*Prostate cancer is no laughing matter,*
R	*Reappearing out of the thinnest air.*
O	*One has surgery eighteen years earlier,*
S	*So it is a shock when it reappears —*
T	*To think it can lie dormant for so long*
A	*And is just lying around, ready to*
T	*Take possession of the skeletal bones,*
E	*Ending my life — a shout, not a whimper!*
C	*Cancer! — we are fighting you tooth and nail —*
A	*Although it is true there are times like this,*
N	*Now for me, when the facts seem dour indeed —*
C	*Causing panic and unrelenting pain,*
E	*Each day praying for the ending to come,*
R	*Rejoicing that I'm still Your much-blessed child!*

Bernalillo, NM, January 16, 2018

His final poem, "The Sun," was written a day later. Some of his earliest poems, written in England, had religious subjects, as did his last verses. He had come full circle.

"The Sun"
an octet poem

The sun shines brightly in the sky—
Giving light to all the earth—
Making plants thrive and grow
Food for animals—
Also for man
To prosper
And thank
God.

Bernalillo, NM, January 17, 2018

During the last three weeks of his life, his visitors were neighbors who were friends to both Will and me, members of the clergy who administered spiritually to him, and Matt, a member of the men's book club. One day, close to the end of Will's life, Matt was just leaving as I entered the room. Will said excitedly to me, "Don't let Matt go. He's the only one who can keep me from the gates of hell!" I did not have the opportunity to ask Matt what had led to that outburst.

Will remained extremely restless the remainder of the day. I stayed a little later than usual, just in case. To try to help him emotionally, I picked up the hymnal I had brought from home and began singing some hymns to comfort him: "The King of Love My Shepherd Is," "Fairest Lord Jesus," "Breathe on Me, Breath of God," "Come Down, O Love Divine." Will listened at first, then turned away from me. I asked, "Shall I continue? Does singing help?" His answer was, "No. Your voice is past it."

I said good night and left. The next day, when I told him that he had hurt my feelings, he had no response. However, he asked me three questions that day, which revealed to me that he was closer to death. The first, "Who is that person standing in the closet doorway?" There was no one I could see. The second, "Who are those people looking at us from the other side of the wall?" "Do you know them?" I asked. "No." The third, "Do you see the wall moving up to the ceiling light?" That was the last of our oral communication.

The next morning, having alerted friends not to visit, I arrived early. The manager of the facility, a friendly, attractive young lady, told me that Will had had a very bad night. He had stood up in bed, had demanded to be taken to the hospital, and had needed to be medically subdued. He was better this morning, she said, and had apologized to her for his behavior and had remarked, "I'm glad that I had the chance to get to know you." Evidently he cared to the end what others thought about the "public" Will.

Throughout the day, I ministered to him as he lay in fever. The oxygen machine, set at its highest output, could not supply what his body needed. I alternated between moistening his feverish lips with a swab and putting the nasal oxygen inserts directly on the lips of his open mouth. He did not look at me during the day or indicate that he wanted to communicate. He did, however, speak briefly with the clergy who visited in the late afternoon.

After the father had left, Will began to jerk violently and sporadically. I held one of his hands securely and chanted over and over, "Lord have mercy, Christ have mercy, Lord have mercy."

Around 6:00 PM an attendant came into the room and said to me, "He's dying. Time to remove the nasal inserts." Will was staring with eyes wide open, looking terrified. As I removed the inserts, he violently jerked one final time. The attendant walked to the window and opened it, saying, "The soul sometimes escapes through the window." She left me alone with his body.

I sat there with conflicting feelings. I was glad that the suffering for him was over, and the anxiety of his impending death for me, but I still wanted him to reach out to me, to explain why he had hidden so many of his feelings from me.

It was hours before I could leave. First the medical examiner had to come, then the mortician, the hospice care worker, the manager of the home, and finally a resident member of the clergy. When I finally got back to my home in Santa Fe, I called Dora in California. She had said good-bye to Will on the phone shortly before he died, and he had nodded at hearing her voice.

Dora expressed how glad she was with having visited him, along with Sue, for a few days after Christmas. Dora and Sue had flown into Albuquerque. I had driven them from the airport to the care home, where Will joyfully greeted them. Although I was in the room throughout their visit, Will completely ignored me. Dora and Sue didn't appear to notice this. During the visit, Will wanted to play Scrabble. Since Sue had never played the game, I helped her to learn the tricks of the game, becoming her partner rather than being a player on my own. Together we won.

The next day we each brought Will gifts—Dora and I gave him pajamas, and Sue presented him with a collection of family pictures of "Grandpa," which she had made into a booklet. Nothing could have pleased him more. Later that day, when we left for the airport, the final good-byes were heartbreaking, both for them and for Will. I stood by.

After driving Dora and Sue to the airport, I returned to Will's room instead of going directly home. In spite of his having ignored me, I had decided to surprise him by an unexpected visit. This time he didn't ignore me. We talked about Dora and Sue for a while, and then I put on my coat to go home.

"Stay here tonight," Will said. "You can lie next to me here on the bed." Perhaps he intended to at last share some of his feelings with me. Unfortunately, I responded with reasons for not staying: I had not left lights on at home; Lovey needed care—food, water, his sandbox changed; neither of us would sleep well; he needed to rest.

"Will you at least kiss me?" he asked. I walked to his bedside and gave him a light kiss on the lips; he did not reach out to touch me. I said, "When I was a child, I was taught to say a nighttime prayer that frightened me. I still include it in my nighttime prayers, but now it comforts me." I recited it:

Now I lay me down to sleep;
I pray Thee, Lord, my soul to keep.
If I should die before I wake,
I pray Thee, Lord, my soul to take."

I asked him, "Did you say that prayer as a child?" He smiled slightly and shook his head *no*. I waved good-bye and left. A tender time like this never returned.

Chapter 13

STAGES OF GRIEF

A week before Will died on February 5, 2018, at the age of eighty-five, I had met with a representative of a funeral home/crematorium from Albuquerque. I had paid for the final expenses to include a private family service at the home before the body was to be cremated. Dora and I had agreed that we would both like to see Will at rest. While Vince and Dora were on their way to Santa Fe, I made the arrangements for the viewing.

Since Will would be cremated in a casket, I chose a cloth-covered composition one of blue; the top would open only for the upper-third portion of the body while a large bouquet of various-colored flowers would cover the remainder of the cover. I had chosen two green plants to be placed on pedestals on either side of the coffin. I agreed to take to the funeral parlor my choice of attire for Will: khaki pants, his favorite tan corduroy jacket, a dress shirt he had liked, and his Deacon's School tie.

On February 10 when Dora, Vince, and I walked into the small private viewing room, Will looked peacefully asleep. He had been bathed and shaved, and his hair had been washed and combed. My last vision of him with mouth open and eyes staring in fright was now replaced with that of a man who was no longer in a struggle to live. Dora read a few excerpts from the Bible, Vince took pictures, and I stood by the casket.

When the attendant came in, I asked him to explain the next procedures. The cremation would take place four days later, allowing time for surgical removal of Will's pacemaker. Will would be cremated in the casket, along with his clothes and the bouquet of flowers. The date of the cremation would be February 14, which ironically fell in 2018 on Valentine's Day and Ash Wednesday. Two days later, Dora and Vince would celebrate their thirty-third wedding anniversary. It would also be the fifty-eighth anniversary of Dora's conception during the Squaw Valley skiing weekend for Will and me.

For the next three months, I was too busy to be mired in grief. Louise, a friend for fifty-five years, since our early teaching days, had died in early December and had left me as the trustee of her estate. I had helped her in 2000 at the time of the death of her close companion, followed six months later by the death of her only child. We had been frequent visitors to each other's houses throughout the years; in her later years, she had often stayed with Will and me for long periods in Manteca.

Her estate had been large, but her California lawyer was neither well organized nor trustworthy. After repeated difficulty in communicating with him, I hired my own lawyer in Santa Fe to help me deal with the estate. Paying bills, gathering information, dealing with forms for business and healthcare, refunds, selling stocks, paying taxes all became part of my life. Meanwhile, I was dealing with Will's papers, records, and finances as well.

During Will's final year of life, I had been the president of a women's group at the church. In addition to overseeing activities and planning for the 2017–18 year, I prepared a series of lectures on the Psalms for our monthly meetings. I had begun working on these during the summer, researching historical sources, studying the Old Testament, taking notes, and arranging the materials into chapters. I planned to provide handouts from five to ten pages, as needed, for each of the lectures. Because Will did not like my using *his* computer, he stood behind me or sat in a chair close by. If I asked him for computer help too often, he insisted on taking over. Will had selected a password for his computer that he would not share with me. However, he finally had to give it to me when he needed to have the transfer made from his home computer to his laptop in December. When he was no longer at home, I prepared the handouts by myself, occasionally needing to call a family member for help. Little by little I learned to become more "computer-wise."

During early May, I needed to plan the details for Will's memorial service, which would be held on Saturday, June 2, at the church, with a noontime reception following in the parish hall. Although the hospitality committee would take care of all the physical arrangements for the reception and provide the majority of the food and drinks, I decided to order special sandwiches from a local bistro, enough to provide for the reception and for a later gathering of family members at my home.

It was important to me to try to achieve an aura of spirituality, beauty, and love as we acknowledged Will's life and death. Will and I had been married for fifty-seven years and had set examples of companionship for others to follow. This was the final occasion to portray Will as he wanted others to remember him – as a husband, father and grandfather, and friend; a seeker of secular and spiritual knowledge; a poet and musician; a former aeronautical engineer, computer programmer, and mathematician; and above all, an Englishman.

The bulletin for the service needed my input. I confirmed Will's choices of the choral anthem "God So Loved the World" by Stainer and my chant-like composition of "The Lord's Prayer," which Will had sung at the close of my second master's recital. I approved of his selection of hymns, including "The King of Love My Shepherd Is," the first hymn I had sung to Will the evening he was so agitated in the care home. The gospel lesson he had chosen was John 10: 11–16: Jesus said, "I am the good shepherd . . . I have other sheep that are not of this fold." This belief, of other sheep being saved, had been the cornerstone of his mother Laura's religious views.

I had chosen a picture of Will to be placed at the end of the bulletin. Taken the day of Dora's wedding, Will was standing in front of a row of books in our Los Gatos home. He looked eternally handsome in a gray tuxedo with a carnation in his buttonhole. The opposite page of the bulletin contained a biographical sketch I had written, ending with, "God bless Will today and always."

When I had finished the preparation for the service and had presented my final lecture on the Psalms on May 15, I had just thirteen days before Dora and Sue would arrive. I suddenly had time for the emotions that I had kept bottled up. I surprised myself when I was overwhelmed with anxiety and panic. I couldn't sleep for days; at times I couldn't breathe. One night I called the ambulance to take me to the hospital. I couldn't sleep there either. The second day they put automatic muscle massagers on my legs and gave me sleep medication at night. I was released to go home the next morning.

Before Dora and Sue arrived a few days later, I had time to read a few books and articles about grief. I learned that when a death has been anticipated, the one left behind can feel physically and emotionally exhausted. I had not realized how exhausted I had become until my frantic activity had ceased.

Dora and Sue stayed in the house with me to give me company and to help me to prepare for the next events. While they were with me, Sue handled meals, calls, and emails. I gave Dora one of the articles on grief I had read, knowing that she was experiencing deep feelings of loss for her father. Dora had brought with her twenty condolences that she had received from friends and relatives. One of the messages to her was from her daughter Sara: "He loved *you* more than anything in this world. He was so proud of you. He adored you to pieces and you got all the best pieces of him." This one hurt me. I knew that it was true, but I had yet to learn how to live with the truth. I felt that I needed to share with Dora a stack of sixty condolences sent to me, most including personal notes indicating that I had been well-liked, even loved, by relatives and friends, along with Will. As Dora read through some of these, I sensed her realization that she had sometimes misjudged me.

Family members arrived in groups: the rest of Dora's family (Vince, Robbie, Sara, and her husband from California); my sister, Nancy, and her family (one daughter from Texas, a second daughter and grandson from California); Maggie came alone from Nebraska.

All went well the day of the memorial. The service was well attended. It was a beautiful, spiritual event— the music was glorious; the sermon, prepared by Father Andrew, captured the earthly Will and his immediate family, along with the encouragement to look ahead to the eternal. Then we all gathered in the memorial garden as Will's ashes were put into his niche in the columbarium.

Dora, Sue, and Maggie had helped me to set up a memorial table of pictures, albums, and items representing Will's life. The food tables had been arranged in the shape of a cross and had been decorated with flowers. I had hired a pianist to play light classical music and tunes from musicals during the reception, providing the right atmosphere for relaxed conversation.

It was a beautiful June day for the family gathering at my home. The garden had been planted with colorful flowers along the front path and in various pots. Most of the family chose to enjoy their refreshments in the garden. The next morning my sister Nancy and her family left; later in the day, Dora and her family said good-bye. Maggie stayed with me an extra day to ease me into my world of being alone again. In the coming months, she called me daily from Nebraska to see how I was doing and to encourage me to share my feelings.

After the family had left, I had more time for reflection. Will and I had had a strained relationship throughout most of our marriage. We had been such different personality types. He was a mathematician, a fact-finder; I was a romantic. He lacked sensitivity;

I was too sensitive. He constantly sought new information; I was goal-oriented. He had been allowed to become a self-centered child; I had learned to share with two sisters. My grief seemed to be centered on our differences.

A friend of mine suggested to me that writing about my thoughts and memories would help me to release my emotions and feelings. However, I needed a focus for writing, and after much thought, I decided to put together a collection of family poems (mainly Will's) in chronological order. For each poem, I planned to include my memory of the occasion that had prompted the poem. In my search for information, I found many of Will's poems on the computer, some in an early book of poems, some tucked away in albums, drawers, reference books, etc. I found not only what I had been looking for but notes, expressions, and articles written by Will, or researched by him. I had not set out to become a detective for the Will I could not find in life, but much of what I found was disturbing to me. I realized that I could not share much of this material with Dora or the grandchildren, who had rose-colored memories of Will. Furthermore, I did not want to disturb those memories.

I changed the focus for my writing. I decided to use Will's poems in chronological order as a basis for my *memoirs* of him and our marriage of fifty-seven years, and to tell my story through the fictional character of Beth. I began writing in October, the anniversary of Will's eighty-fifth birthday. As I released my anger toward Will and my own feelings of guilt, I began to understand what I had really been grieving for*: a loving marriage that had not existed, except for a brief early time.*

When I accepted the realization that love had so often been missing from our marriage, I began to take responsibility for *my* part in it. I reminded myself that I had chosen to marry a charming Englishman, and I had chosen to stay with him even when I found him to be increasingly self-centered and secretive—the "public" and the "private" Will. These attributes had led him more and more into the world of isolation and estrangement from me. However, in spite of all of the changes that had taken place in our fifty-seven years together, we had remained friends until the last months of his life, when he was losing control of everything.

Furthermore, I had to take responsibility for my cruel remark to him: "I want you to know that you have deprived me of a life of love." There was truth in the deprivation of intimate love, of kissing, fondling, hugging, touching, and comforting. But my life had been full of love—the love of God, a child and grandchildren from Will, the love and fulfillment of music, the beauty and love of nature, the love of my American family and friends, the love of Will's father, and on and on and on.

God had twice given me life—when I was born and when I was allowed to return to raise Dora. And God was not yet through with my life.

Conclusion

*N*ow that Will is gone, I am beginning to change many of my ways of living. I can sit down at the piano and play without wondering if he is hearing me. I can listen to romantic music, which he never liked. I can communicate more freely with Dora, Sue, and Robbie. Unlike Will, I like to exercise and participate in programs at the gym, including dance, which enlivens my day. I retain my old interests as well — reading, writing, attending church, communicating with friends, and traveling.

I am no longer on a quest to find the "real Will" or to try to better understand him. Perhaps a more complete understanding will occur after my death. Although our earthly relationship has ended, I am a believer that God allows us to continue to develop our love for each other after death, ultimately reaching an understanding of LOVE itself.

A month after Will died, I felt compelled to write a poem about him. At the time, I didn't completely understand what I had written. Now I do.

How Did I Not Know?
To Will

How did I not know,
Until your breathing ceased
That I loved you so?

At first I loved your wit,
Your smile, your English ways,
Your quick wink for me alone.
Then our natures grew
And joined to make us one.
That was love, we knew.

How did we not know,
Then that love is ever changing,
Rearranging each of us?
That sorrow and trouble come and go,
And sometimes joy replaces woe.

Did love yet remain
When we grew old together?
Familiar habits, words and ways
Were second nature now—
A tiresome verse, a tale retold,
A body frail from being old.

How did I not know,
That when your breathing ceased,
Your frame at last released
From misery and pain,
I would shout, "Not yet, Lord, not yet!"

But love thinks not of self alone;
The gift of memory remains.
So, I am here, and you are gone
To peace and joy forevermore,
For God is LOVE,
And love goes on.

ABOUT THE AUTHOR:

*F*auneil was born and raised in northeastern Nebraska. She has four college degrees: BSc in Education from the University of Nebraska; MEd from the University of Arizona; BA and MA in music from San Jose State University. She has traveled extensively throughout the U.S., Europe, and Canada. She has had two careers, as an English teacher and as a professional musician, both described in her writing.

CPSIA information can be obtained
at www.ICGtesting.com
Printed in the USA
FSHW012111230819
61355FS